WHAT THE HELL HAPPENED TO ME?!

What the HELL Happened to Me?!

SAM HUMPHREY

Inspirit Alliance

What the HELL Happened to Me?!

Copyright © 2022 samuel c humphrey

Cover design by: sam humphrey
www.sidecarsam.com

Extra Fotos Edition

ISBN: 978-1-959239-03-1
Library of Congress Control Number: 2022915535

Printed in the United States of America

What the HELL Happened to Me?!

by sam humphrey

Contents

For Cindy Lou
Thank you for keeping me alive.

Preface

I was born in Moscow, Idaho. My family moved to Germany shortly thereafter, where we lived for four years. Two sisters were born there. After that we spent a year in Japan, where a third sister was born. We moved back to the Inland Northwest United States after that. I lived there until I graduated High School. I joined the U.S. Navy right out of High School, did four years there, got out and went to a Commercial Dive school just south of Seattle. I have been a Commercial Diver ever since. While pursuing my Dive Career, I went back to college (university) and earned a B.S. in Biology. I started riding motorized two-wheelers when I was eight. I bought my first - a Montgomery Wards Moped - when I was thirteen. At sixteen I was riding a Honda 125 Enduro. While in the Navy I bought a Honda CX500, my very first Brand New Motorcycle. Since then I have owned many Motorcycles and still do. In June of 2018 I was in a Catastrophic Motorcycle Accident that left me a Paraplegic in a wheelchair.

I used to Live Life on the Edge

I Fell Off and Headed for the Abyss

Good Souls Helped Me Back

Section One

What the HELL Happened to ME?!

A Motorcycle Accident and Beyond

Chapter 1

I had been visiting my friend, Doug, east of Birmingham, Alabama. See, I was working on the Olmsted Dam project on the Ohio River just outside of Paducah, Kentucky. It was an ongoing project that I had been involved with for several years. We routinely got Weekends and Holidays off. I liked having my Bike with me so I could go for rides during my off time. Also, I'd rather drive to work than fly when I work out of town. I like to see where I am going. You know, Motorcyclist, "getting there is half the fun." Plus, I could do more traveling from there when my hitch was up (typically four weeks on, four weeks off).

It's roughly seventeen hundred miles from my house in Helena, Montana to Paducah. I would
usually take just over a day to make that trip, spending the night in Iowa somewhere, like Hamburg. Anyway, I had been in Paducah about a week, maybe two, into this hitch and we got Friday, Saturday, and Sunday off. I figured this was a perfect

opportunity to see Doug. I texted him and asked what he was up to for the weekend and he said a little town near him was having "Burger Wars" that weekend and there would be lots of good Burgers, Beer, and other Adult Beverages. Sounds like a Blast to me! I'm in. Doug was gracious enough to let me crash at his place, so I beat feet down to southeastern Alabama Friday morning.

Of course, I had to take a few Foto Ops along the way! I hit some

traffic in Tennessee, but the weather was wonderful. It was sunny and the temperature was just right to be comfortable wearing my Leather Jacket. I was also wearing my

Full-Face Helmet. I didn't always wear a Helmet, but in the Southern States they have Helmet Laws, so I did. Besides there were quite a few Bugs out and I didn't want any more on my teeth than I already had! I took more Fotos. I was in no hurry to get anywhere. I didn't need to check into any Motel, just get to Doug's house. He told me there was a big metal Frog near his house. Cindy loves Frogs, so I was keeping an eye out for it. Doug's place wasn't very far from the Frog. I can't tell you how far. I don't remember. Besides I never pay much attention to Miles or Time when I am riding for fun – which is almost ALL the time I am on a Bike! Ha ha!

"Not very far" could be anything less than Three Hundred Miles for me. I got to Doug's in the late afternoon/early evening. His place is Fabulous! Lots of space, lots of greenery, trees and a creek. It is beautiful. We didn't do anything too fancy for dinner. I don't remember what we ate, something good, maybe grilled. We drank Beer too. He wanted to get to the Hamburger Wars fairly early as he had family working at least one of the

Booths. We drank and talked and had a great time. I don't remember how late we stayed up, but I do know I slept really well. We got up at a reasonable hour – not particularly early. Definitely not Beemer Early! Doug's Brother-in-Law, Bryan, was with us and we were going to go to the Burger Wars then do a little riding around the area afterwards. I didn't have to be to work until Monday afternoon so I had plenty of time to ride back to Paducah on Sunday. We hopped on our machines and headed to the little town, Opelika (Creek for "Large Swamp"), where the Burger Wars were taking place. When we got there, I was surprised by how many Booths were set up. The weather was nice.

It was perfect when we got there, but got a little warm in the afternoon. That's okay because we planned on spending the afternoon riding around and looking at the sites. Good company and good fun. I think I had Eight different types of Burgers. I don't remember any Milkshakes. I think I mostly drank Water, but I do remember going into a Brew House and checking it out. We weren't drinking because we were planning on riding in the latter part of the day. Mostly Doug was just showing me around the great little town of Opelika. Everybody was very friendly. As you can see by my Belly, I eat plenty of Hamburgers and drink my fair share of Beer!

Sorry Doug and Jason, but I can't remember what University that Tiger belongs to. Is it Roll tide? or am I going to get punched?! Ha ha. Just recently got a note from Doug and the Tiger belongs to Auburn University – !! WAR EAGLE !! Thank you, Doug.

We got back on our Bikes and went riding. It was warm if you were milling around, but it made for very comfortable riding. The Scenery was Incredible! Jason likes to call it "God's Country." I always think people are referring to Montana when they say that, but I do have to admit that Alabama holds a close second. It is a beautiful place to ride for sure.

See what I mean? It's beautiful and the weather was great. We spent all afternoon riding. We visited Horseshoe Bend National Military Park, the site of a battle between Andrew Jackson's army and the Red Stick Creek Indians. It was a beautiful park. I remember seeing some Cannons and some of the Battlements. We were there after the park officially closed and almost got locked in. We also went to a restaurant on Lake Martin, Kowaliga (like the Hank Williams' song) Restaurant, that had a Wooden Indian in the reception area. We wanted to roll our Indians in so we could take a Foto of "An Indian by an Indian" for the IndianRider.net site, but the employees said "No Way!" We took a Foto of ourselves next to the Indian instead. If I remember correctly,

we got back to Doug's place right around Sunset. I'm not real sure, my memory of that weekend is a little fuzzy. We drank Beer, more than the previous night because none of us had anywhere to be the next day really. I think we did some kind of Bar-B-Que for dinner and I think other people may have come over. I have vague recollections of other people around, but I wouldn't bet my life on who or when. All I do know for sure is we had a Fabulous time because Doug and his family are good people and great hosts. I remember us talking quite a bit about lots of things. We were reminiscing about a recent trip we had made to Nashville. We all met there, Doug and Bryan, and Jason with his better half, Jeannie (they came in a Cage though. Shame, shame. Just kidding Jason. Ha!), and we met a couple other people there, one from Australia the other from Chicago. We were there to see Poison. They were supposed to play at an open air arena and their Drummer is a member of the IndianRider.net group. He also rides a

Norton Commando. I was hoping to touch base with him so we could practice our Brit accents as we talked about our "Snortin' Nortons!" No such luck though. It was fairly wet that weekend. The concert kept getting cancelled when it would rain, then back on when the storm clouds went away, and besides that our concert got Trumped! Yes, Trump was making a surprise visit to Nashville for some political thing. Roads got shut down and that caused the concert to be cancelled for sure in the end. Bum Donuts Big Time! We were bummed we didn't get to see Poison, but we still had a good time. We went Barhopping in Nashville. We drank Irish Car Bombs in one bar, and ended up at the Big Bang on Broadway. They had Dueling Piano Players there. We had plenty to drink and did a fair amount of dancing if I remember correctly.

We had a Blast! We all got to see Jason and Jeannie's new car too! Well that was just reminiscing. It was fun times and it's these kind of times I miss the most. I really want to do something about getting back on a Sidecar Rig. I have some ideas.

Doug remembers us also talking about previous wrecks and old "war wounds." I think we talked until we couldn't keep our eyes open anymore. I know I slept really well that night. I was full of good Food, good Beer, and conversation with good Friends. I remember waking up feeling refreshed and ready to ride. I was looking forward to a nice leisurely ride on the back roads to Paducah. I only ride the main Highways when there is no other choice or I need to get somewhere in a timely manner.

Chapter 2

Sunday morning, pushing noon if I remember correctly, we got up and had a little breakfast. I am all packed up and ready to go. The weather is Fabulous; Blue Sky and warm! Giving Hugs and telling each other to "Take Care" and "we will keep in touch and get together again soon." Little did we know what the future had in store. I guess you never know. You just go with the flow and keep your head above water as best you can. Anyway, I jumped on my Bike, waved, and was off. Highway 431 looked like a nice way north and I had never been on that road before. It wasn't one of the main roads north, or maybe it was, it just had less traffic than the main highway from Birmingham to Nashville and beyond. I remember the Blue Sky and a nice paved road with not too much traffic. I think I rode through a couple small towns. It did seem like there were a lot of Asphalt Snakes on this highway though. Around a hundred and fifty miles later I decided to get fuel. I saw a Gas Station up the road on the far right corner of an intersection. The traffic was stopped and there were Cop cars and a couple Ambulances blocking the intersection. The Police were guiding people through the intersection one at a time. I got to the Gas Station and filled my tank. There were a couple other Motorcycle Riders there getting fuel too. We greeted each other and talked a little about where we were riding that day. Two of them were members of a Women's riding group.

Perhaps I should have looked at that accident as Foreshadowing? I don't know. How would you know? Things always look different when you look back on them. "Hindsight is 20/20" isn't that what they say? I tend to look forward and not back. When something is done, it is done, and there is no way you can go back and undo it. You just have to live with it and move forward. Hopefully you learn from it and don't make the same mistakes again. And then again sometimes you do. My Grandma Mildred never wanted me on Motorcycles in the first place. She was really hoping that I would have quit riding after my first serious accident back in 1982 when I spent six weeks in the hospital. But, Nooooo, as soon as I was able, I was right back on my bike. I got it repaired and kept on riding.

Again, in 1994 I was in another Catastrophic Motorcycle Accident. I like saying that "Catastrophic Motorcycle Accident." It sounds so menacing, or something, or, I don't know, Catastrophic! Ha! Even though I like the sound of "Catastrophic" doesn't mean that I like being involved in anything Catastrophic. That time I hit the rear wheel of a car so hard that the rear tire popped off the rim. It also bent the front forks of my Shadow 1100. The girl driving the car had slowed down and veered to the right. I saw a dirt road off to the right just up ahead. Stupid me, I assumed she was turning right. Instead, no blinker, no hand sign, no warning, she turned Left. I had veered left to pass her as she was making her "right turn" so had also sped up a little. Instead, she turned left. My last thought was "Oh man, this is probably gonna hurt." I don't remember any pain. I don't remember hitting her car. I don't remember flying through the air like a Human Cannonball. I just remember thinking it wasn't going to be good and slamming on my brakes. The next thing I remember seeing is all black with a bunch of red, grinning, gibbering faces encircling me. Am I in Hell, or what? A few seconds later the faces morphed into full bodies and I saw Blue Sky framed by bright green pine tree tops. I was heading north to Priest Lake from Coeur D' Alene on Highway 41 through Spirit Lake, Idaho. I was still laying in the middle of the Highway; people were all around me. Someone had put a cushion under my head. They were all asking if I was alright. I said I was and just wanted to know where my Bike was and what shape it was in. They wouldn't let me get up. They told me an ambulance was on the way. Shit, I didn't want to pay for any ambulance ride. I wanted to get back on my Bike and get to Priest Lake. We were wasting time here. A County Sheriff showed up at the same time the ambulance did. The paramedics checked me over and said I appeared fine, but wanted to take me to the hospital anyway. I got up and felt okay. My head hurt a little. One of the witnesses told the Sheriff that I went flying over the car after hitting it and landed on my head about twenty feet away. The Sheriff asked me where my Helmet was. I told him it was strapped to the backseat of my Motorcycle. "That's a good place for it!" he replied. There was an eight-foot-long skid mark from my rear tire in the middle of the road. My Bike was at the side of the road upright and on its kickstand. The front disc was bent and wouldn't let the front wheel spin all the way around. It looks like I won't be riding this bike until I make a few repairs. The Forks had bent back so bad that there was an imprint from the Radiator Grill on the front Fender. The Sheriff asked me if I wanted a tow truck. I told him no, and asked if he would call my dad to ask him to bring his truck out so we could haul my Bike back to my House. He could radio the Sheriff Station and have someone call my dad. He said "Okay" and left me to myself on the side of the road. Everybody left. The Sheriff called my dad. My dad showed up four hours later with my wife and little daughter. They were freaked out. My head really hurt and I was starting to have double vision. My dad brought my motorcycle ramp – an eight-foot long two-by-ten with two two-by-fours screwed onto one face. I unbolted the front disc from the wheel and rode my Bike up into the bed of my dad's pickup. I told him I thought I should go to the hospital. My head really hurt and my double vision was getting worse. We went to the Emergency Room at Deaconess Hospital in Spokane, about two hours from where I wrecked my Bike. They looked me over, gave me two aspirin and told me to call them in the morning if I was still feeling bad. I went home and lay down. I went to sleep. When I woke up in the morning my head still really hurt, maybe a little less than the night before, but my double vision was just as bad if not worse. I felt kind of sick to my stomach. I went back to the Emergency Room. They called a Neurologist this time. He checked me out, did a Cat Scan, and got really angry. He asked me about my visit to the Emergency Room the night before. Next he called the Hospital director and started yelling about the Emergency Room staff. He told me my skull was cracked in half right between my eyes. My brain was swelling and I could have, should have, died overnight. He did say, that now, about twenty-four hours after the accident, I had made it through the dangerous time and I would live. That was good news! I lost my sense of smell and taste though. It took two years before I got those senses back and I'm still only about eighty or ninety percent. I can't smell people's farts. so that's a good thing! My family was hoping I was done with Motorcycles after that accident. Are you Kidding Me?! I just gotta fix that Pony and get right back on her. I rebuilt her back better and faster than she was before and kept on riding. Anyway, back to Alabama and 2018. It was Sunny and warm. The road was pretty good and there wasn't much traffic. It was a great day for riding and it looked like I would have a great ride back to Paducah. After filling my tank with gas, cramming down a hotdog. and drinking a bottle of water, I got back on the road. A little ways down the road, I have Zero recollection of how far, I saw a pile of vintage Hearses and Ambulances off to the left. I pulled over. I LOVE vintage Hearses and Ambulances. I used to own a 1962 Cadillac Ambulance. It was an awesome vehicle. I bought it before Ghostbusters the movie came out and owned it when that movie hit the theaters. Of course, I had to paint the Ghostbusters' Logo on the back of it. That was the vehicle I was driving around when I went to college the first time – where I learned to be a Commercial Diver. We had to SCUBA dive at least once a month then and my Ambulance was the perfect vehicle to take a bunch of crazy college students SCUBA diving. Anyway, I love vintage Ambulances, so I had to pull over and check these out. Of course, I had to take a Foto or five of my Bike next to this pile of vintage rigs too.

The Haunted Chicken House! WHAT?! That is so Awesome! I had to visit it and see what it was all about. The place was off the Highway on a dirt road, that was actually somewhat muddy. I saw a sign that said they were closed and I didn't want to get my nine-hundred-pound Scooter stuck in the mud so I opted not to go search it out. Besides these Ambulances and Hearses were Kool. A little sad that they weren't in drive-able condition though. These are the last Fotos I ever took while on a ride. Again, maybe it was a little Foreshadowing. I will never know. Or maybe I will when I finally leave this earth! I didn't see it that way then, though. I was just enjoying the day, enjoying the ride and having fun taking Fotos of my Bike next to interesting roadside attractions.

Little did I know these would be the last and it still brings tears to my eyes when I think about that. There are So many more places where I wanted to take Fotos of my Motorcycle. After taking these Fotos, I got back on my Bike and headed North to Kentucky. Really, I have Zero recollection of how far I went from here. My next memory after stopping here is of the handlebars going into Tank-Slapping Mode. If you've never experienced that, I hope you never do. Sometimes you can pull out of it, sometimes you can't. This time I couldn't.

Chapter 3

Riding down the road, or is it "up the road" when you are heading north? I don't know. My mind wanders a lot when I ride. I think of all kinds of things. Ponder life, love, the afterlife, all kinds of things, do I need to pee? The Sun was out, it was warm, the riding was exceptional. I don't think I've ever seen this many Asphalt Snakes on a Highway before. Except maybe that section of Route 66 in Missouri (pronounced Misery) that is closed off to traffic. I rode my bike on it once even though it was closed to the public. I did that a fair amount. Just because a road is closed doesn't mean it is closed to Motorcycles! You should see where I used to take my IMZ Ural! Blue Skies, Warm Pavement, Soft Asphalt Snakes. I'm cruising along about Sixty mph. I think the speed limit was Fifty-Five. I usually ride Five over. My most comfortable cruising speed on my Indian is Eighty-Five to Ninety. Of course, that changes with the road, road conditions, and the weather. And group rides. Oh boy, don't get me started on Group Rides. I'm not real good at them. Nobody, or not many, ride like I do. Anyway, the Indian just purrs and kind of floats along the road at that speed and you really go through the miles. I'd stop every couple hours for gas, a snack and a Monster Moco Loco, usually taking fifteen minutes or less for my stop. I'd hit the head (bathroom) if I needed too. So here I am cruising along at sixty. Traffic is light and I have the Cruise Control on, Left hand on the handlebars, the Right one is on my thigh. Life is good. I look up and smile at the sun. The median is covered in bright Green Grass about a meter (three feet) high. That looks like a soft spot for a landing. I'll bet the ground in the median there is soft, wet mud. It rains a lot in Alabama so it is very Green and there is Mud everywhere. I always look at the sides of the roads and medians when I ride. You never know when you might need a soft landing or some kind of escape route. You can never depend on the Cage drivers to do the right thing. You wouldn't believe the things I have seen people do while they were driving their cars down the road. Talking on the Cell Phone is nothing! If only that were the worst thing I've seen. But I digress, traffic is light and I am really enjoying my ride. Up ahead I see a Station Wagon in the right lane. I am in the right lane also. The left lane is for passing, not driving, especially not driving the speed limit or less. It is for Passing. I could go off on that subject too, but I won't. I am enjoying my ride and I am full of Good and Happy thoughts. The Station Wagon is cruising along about fifty I think. That's okay, it's in the right lane. People should drive the speeds they are comfortable with. I am coming up on it fairly quickly. I am conscious of a Pickup Truck pacing me and we have passed several cars in the last few miles. I turn on my Blinker and pull into the left lane. I twist my throttle to speed up to sixty-five or so. I don't like to have traffic beside me if I can help it. Like I said, you never know what the Cage is going to do. I always assume the worst. I usually ride with the idea that everybody on the road is out to run me over. Sometimes that is true, I've even had drivers pull a gun on me as I passed them. I guess they were pissed because their ratty old rig wouldn't go as fast as my bike. Or maybe they were jealous because I was on a Bike and they weren't. See what I mean? Lots of things go through my mind when I ride. Passing this beige Station Wagon, I notice it is a younger Brunette driving. She seems to be paying attention to the road even though there are a couple kids in the back seat. As I pass, she speeds up a little. I speed up a little. She speeds up a little more. This really irritates me when people do that. I look at her and she looks at me. I shake my head "no" and she slows back down. I don't think she was consciously speeding up, People do that subconsciously sometimes, keep pace with other vehicles around them without really thinking about it. I was not angry, upset, or even peeved a little with her. She seemed to be driving responsibly. I slow down a little but keep passing her getting ready to pull back into the right lane. I am back down to sixty-five mph when all of a sudden my Handlebars start flopping side to side really hard. Oh Dammmn! Tank Slapper. That is when your Handlebars flop side to side so far that the grips hit the gas tank, hence "Tank Slapper." That used to be a lot more common on older bikes. Mostly English and German bikes. I don't hear of it happening on Jap Bikes much. And it's even rarer on the heavy bikes like Harleys, Indians, or the Boss Hoss! I can barely remember the last time this happened to me. It was on one of my smaller Beemers and all I had to do was slow down a little and stiff arm the handlebars. I don't have this issue on the Ural or my 1968 BMW R50 because they have a twist knob on the top of the Triple Tree that allows me to tighten the tension on the Steering Head Bearings. No such thing on my Indian. At this point I wish it would have had that feature! I roll the throttle forward to shut off the Cruise Control and I try to stiff arm the handlebars, but the Bike is just too heavy and I can't stop the Tank Slapping. My Bike is not slowing, the Cruise Control isn't shutting off. I tap the foot brake on the right side to shut off the Cruise Control and slow the Bike a little. When I move my foot off the the brake I feel the Cruise Control bring the Bike back up to speed. Shit, shit, shit. What is going on. I am going to go down. I'm going to hit the pavement and get run over by that Truck behind me. Am I going to hit the side of the Station Wagon? NO! I will not involve another vehicle in an accident if I can help it. F#&K!!!

Why won't the Cruise Control shut off? Why can't I slow down. I can't let go of the Handlebars, because then they'd really flop and I'd probably get thrown off the bike. Shit. I can't stop the Tank Slapping. Is that Truck gonna hit me? I'm going down. I know it for sure. I'm about to paint the road surface with skin and blood. I don't want to hit the Station Wagon. The Median! Look at that Tall Green Grass! I'll bet the ground is soft and muddy. That wouldn't be a bad landing, might not even beat the Bike up too bad. Maybe I'll be able to pick up the Bike and ride on home after this little episode is over. I think I can veer left and into the median. I'll lean that way and try to push myself into the median. At least I won't hit the Station Wagon or get run over by that Pickup. It's working! I'm in the left emergency parking lane. Good thing there isn't a cable fence lining the median like up in Kentucky. A guy I know in Helena hit the guard rail with his Harley and died on the scene. I did NOT need to be hitting any cable fence or guard rail. Thank you Alabama DOT. Into the Grass. Whew! Holy Shit!! What the Hell is that Concrete Highway Divider doing hiding in the Tall, Soft, Green Grass? Well, there goes my soft landing. That is what was going through my head. All those thoughts in a matter of seconds. I swear it was less than a minute from the time I knew I couldn't stop the Tank Slap and was going down to actually seeing the highway divider even though it seemed like ten or fifteen. In front of me is a Concrete Highway divider more or less perpendicular to the normal way of lining them up. It is surrounded by Tall Green Grass. I see several other Concrete Dividers in the median. They are placed in a spread out herring bone fashion. I suppose it's to slow the water flowing down the median. I was on a slight incline. It rains so much here in Alabama I guess the DOT puts these in the median to slow the erosion. The least they could do is cut the grass so motorists could see the Concrete Blocks. I mean, I thought I had a place for a soft landing, but now I realize I don't. F U Alabama DOT!

The last thought going through my head after seeing that big huge (and getting bigger) Concrete Divider is "Oh, No, This is Gonna Hurt!" I don't remember hitting it or flying through the air. Cue the song "Human Cannonball" by Webb Wilder. I always wanted to be a Human Cannonball in a Circus. I thought it would be fun. The Human Cannonball is one of my favorite songs. I didn't want to be a record-breaking Human Cannonball like David "The Bullet" Smith. I just wanted to be a run of the mill Human Cannonball in between Dive Jobs and good Motorcycle rides. It seemed like it would be fun. Being thrown off a speeding Motorcycle that suddenly stopped is NOT how I wanted to be launched. Besides there was not a landing net or airbag set up for me to land on. If I was lucky, I would land in the tall, soft, green grass in between the Concrete Dividers. Of course I don't remember my flight or my landing. The next thing I remember is someone asking someone else how to get this helmet off his head. I was wearing my Brand New Nolan Full Face Modular Helmet. I had purchased it only a month before. My previous one, seven years old. was kind of worn out. I thought I opened my eyes, but everything was Black, Black as night. Black as the water at four hundred feet with no dive light. "There is a little red button on the chin strap that you push to undo the chin strap" I told the voices. I heard them confirm they found it. I helped them undo it and felt them pull the helmet off my head. Everything is still black. "We need to get you in the Ambulance" they said. "There is no place for the Helicopter to land here so we will need to load you up and drive you to a landing area." I told them that would be fine. I could move my arms. My left shoulder ached. My chest hurt if my right arm was by my side, but the pain went away if I raised my right arm. So I raised my right arm. "What are you doing?!" the voices excitedly asked. "My chest feels better if my arm is raised" I explained. They said that was okay, they could work around that. Still everything is black. I'm pretty sure my eyes were open. It felt like they were anyway. I could feel myself blink. I think my eyes were watering. Then I heard another voice. "Hi Sam, you are Sam Humphrey aren't you?" I replied that I was indeed sam humphrey. "I am Deputy Sheriff (I don't remember his name) and I have your phone here." "Do I have all my Teeth?" I asked. "Are my teeth still in my mouth?" "Yes your teeth look fine," he responded. "I see a phone number for a Cindy Lou Humphrey in your phone. Is that your wife?" He asked. I told him it was. He asked if it was okay to giver her a call and let her know what had happened. I told him that would be great. She would probably want to know how I was and where I was. He said he'd call her then. I didn't hear him call her. Everything was still Black. I felt the paramedics lift me into the ambulance and click me into place. They were talking but I don;t remember what they said. I asked if there was something I could hold on to with my right hand to keep it elevated. They said there wasn't. I just kept my arm raised. I don't know how long I was in the ambulance for. I felt it stop and I heard a helicopter outside the van. I heard the doors open and heard them unhook the gurney. I heard the paramedics talking to the helicopter crew. They asked why my arm was raised. I told them it was more comfortable for me. They asked me to lower it to my side while they transferred me into the helicopter. I complied. Black, everything was still Black. I'm pretty sure my eyes were open. I felt them jostle me around and lean me almost ninety degrees to the left. I must have been strapped in. I envisioned myself strapped into a Stokes Litter and being carried around. I had put enough people into Stokes doing rescue training for my dive jobs. I had never been in one before though. A new experience! Yay! Not really. They got me into the helicopter and I heard the door close. I asked if I could raise my right arm again. They asked why and I told them my chest felt better when it was raised. They told me it would be okay as long as I didn't grab onto anything. I promised I wouldn't. Everything was still Black, Black, Black. I felt and heard the helicopter take off. That is the last thing I remember until I saw Cindy staring at me with a worried look on her face.

Chapter 4

I woke up in a Hospital. I have no idea how long I was in there before my first cognitive thought returned. All I knew is that I couldn't talk and couldn't really move much. I could move my arms about. I had some weird hose thing attached to my face with something stuffed down my throat. WHAT IS GOING ON!?!?! I wanted to scream. But I couldn't. I looked at Cindy and she was looking at me. I could feel her hand on the side of my face.

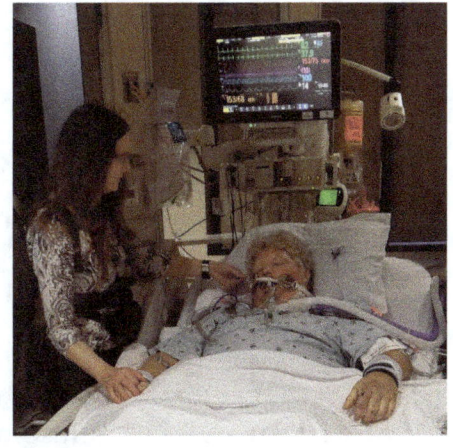

She had a worried look on her face and her eyes were teary. I couldn't ask what was wrong. I indicated for something to write on. It took a while for them to understand what I wanted. I think my sister, Heather, was there too, but I'm not sure. My memory from my time in the Hospital is a little jumbled. I could hear them talking trying to figure out what I wanted. Finally, they gave me a pen and some paper. At last! I could communicate. I'm not sure, but I think the first thing I asked for was a Chocolate Milk! Cindy says I told her we should buy an Indian

Springfield Dark Horse to replace my Chief because, apparently, I said it had better front wheel geometry for sidecars.

Cindy remembers my time in the Hospital much better than I do, but she can't really talk about it. I think she has severe PTSD from that experience. She has really come through for me though. She is the best Nurse, Advocate, Caregiver, Partner that I ever had or could ever wish for. I love her more than she knows. I had a Pen and Paper! I could communicate! I remember asking for a OUIJA Board. That may seem strange to you, but it made perfect sense to me. It had all the letters on it. It had the words Yes, No, Hello, and Goodbye already printed on it. I figured that would make it easier to communicate and wouldn't waste tons of paper. Apparently I thought I had a lot to say. I don't remember ever getting a OUIJA Board. Cindy swears they got one for me, but I never did see it, or at least I don't remember seeing it. Cindy did say the Nurses were a little freaked out or bothered that I had asked for a OUIJA Board. They must have thought I was possessed by a Demon or perhaps Satan himself. I know I can be a Horny Little Devil, but I am not an Evil guy. I remember asking for some other stuff, but don't remember what that was. I do remember seeing some Sympathy cards too, sent from friends and family. The next moment of memory I have, I woke up and the thing on my face was gone. Now I only had a tube thing going around my throat. I still couldn't talk. I later learned that I had a Trach Tube installed now. Still no OUIJA Board, but I did have a White Board and a dry-erase marker, Purple of course! Well, at least I could communicate. I had a beard and somewhat of a mustache when I had my accident. The nursing staff or a doctor or someone wanted to shave part of my beard to do some medical thing I don't know what it was, but I indicated they could do whatever they needed to.

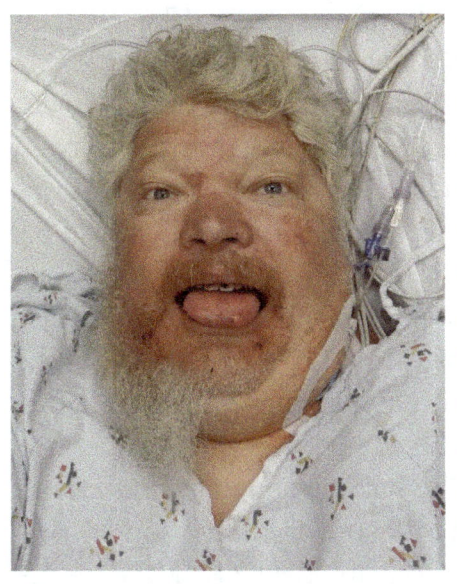

They said they only needed to shave half of it. I tried to convince them to shave the whole thing, to no avail though. They never did shave the other half of my face! I don't need to look anymore like a Clown than I already do! I finally convinced someone to shave the other half of my beard. I don't know who, and I don't remember when, but it was probably Cindy. Next time I saw my face, my teeth were Green and I have no idea why. Is there a toothbrush anywhere? That little face mask was for Oxygen. They wanted me to breathe pure Oxygen on a regular basis, not sure why, my Blood Oxygen level has always been good and I think every time they measured it, it was in the high nineties. I had pretty good insurance coverage, so I'm pretty sure I got extra tests and stuff that I didn't really need. I'll mention more on that later. Cindy was smiling and even laughing with Heather this time I was awake. That made me feel happy. Also made me feel that maybe my situation wasn't too terrible. I still had no idea what the extent of the damage was.

I think I posted that selfie of me with the half-beard on my Facebook page because I remember one of my co-workers saying that my Mustache was Redder than normal. I replied that "It must be the Food and Elevated Oxygen in my Blood. Looking back, I think it was the dried Blood in my Mustache that had colored it Red. Gross. I guess the Nurses didn't clean me up all that well when I first showed up. I think I was in the ICU for Four weeks, maybe three. I don't remember and it doesn't seem like it was that long to me. I do remember waking up a couple times and thinking I was in the Twilight Zone. I mean I REALLY thought I was in the Twilight Zone. My perception of things was really strange. I heard strange voices and sometimes they were warped and twisted sounding. I heard strange sounds. Sometimes my perception of what I was seeing, nurses, Cindy, Heather, would be warped and morphed. I had weird visions and dreams. I couldn't distinguish between my dreams and my perceived reality sometimes. I have always been a Lucid Dreamer, so that probably just added to the weirdness. I remember my sister, Heidi, visiting from Seattle. She was all smiles and happy to see me. She would touch me and kind of stroke or pet me. She had several dogs and I think that was her subconscious way of showing affection or that she cared. I later learned that I broke my back at the T-7 verte-bra, actually demolished that vertebra, and was classified as a T-6/T-7 ASIA 1 Complete Paraplegic. Anyway, what the meant for me was that I had Zero feeling and muscle control from my Breastplate or Nipple Line down. What that doesn't explain is that I have a band of Hyper-Sensitivity that is about 2 inches wide encircling my chest right at that level just above where I have no sensation.

So Heidi would "pet" me and because of my position in bed and all the furniture around my bed, or whatever, she ended up moving her hand back and forth right over that band. It felt like she was sand-ing my skin off with Extra Coarse Sandpaper. I would try to hold her hand to keep her from doing it. I hope she didn't
take that as meaning I didn't appreciate her company and

thoughtfulness. I was glad to have her visit and give Cindy someone to talk to.

I remember my cousin, Jim, visiting me from Virginia. It was good to see him. We had reconnected a couple years earlier when I rode to his house just before the Fourth of July and we went on a Fabulous Motorcycle Ride down the Blue Ridge Parkway. I had visited him over the Fourth the previous year also and was looking for a good ride with him this Fourth of July weekend. The "Best laid plans of Mice and Men." You never know how things are going to play out.

I've always believed that, so I usually don't plan more than a couple days in the future, I just go. We didn't plan our trip down the Blue Ridge. I just showed up and we figured it out from there. Same thing when a friend, Chris, and I planned a trip to Europe. We both bought Motorcycles in Germany off the German E-Bay site. We bought them sight unseen in January and flew to Germany the following May. I took Cindy with me. The only plans we had made for that trip was that it would be four weeks long and we would start the trip at the Town where my bike was. We made One hotel reservation before we left and that was for the night we arrived in Germany. Cindy was nervous about that trip, she was a planner, but we had a great time. The trip went really well and I think I converted Cindy to be a little more Spontaneous. Anyway, Jim visited. It was good to see him and he was glad I was alive. He was really distraught about the accident and couldn't fathom how it had happened. He kept talking about how many miles I had ridden, and how much experience I had, and how this accident occurred on such a small trip. He seemed to just have a hard time wrapping his head around it. He kept asking how it had happened, but I couldn't really explain it. Especially trying to write it all on a White Board with a Purple dry-erase marker! Jim's visit was only a couple days. He had to get back to work. I was glad to see him though.

I think Heidi visited for about a week. I can't really remember and my perception of time was way off. I do remember that she gave Cindy a break and stayed with me overnight so Cindy could go back to the hotel, get showered, and hopefully get a good night's rest. She really couldn't get rest in the ICU. I mean there is noise, lights, and activity twenty-four hours a day, seven days a week. We could hear the helicopters landing on the roof all the time. We could hear the moaning and screaming patients being wheeled in and out of the ICU at all hours. We could hear the crying families in the other rooms. Cindy needed a break. Heidi was happy to stay the night with me. Cindy left in the evening.

In the late evening we heard some U.S. soldiers had been admitted to the ICU. We didn't know what that was about, but the nurses told us that the Hospital security had been increased. Shortly thereafter we heard a bunch of Alarms go off. Then the nursing and staff started running around and talking loudly. Next an announcement came over the Hospital loudspeaker that the Hospital was going into Lockdown! Two orderlies rushed in and transferred me from my bed to a gurney and said they had to get an MRI done and it was an emergency because the Hospital had been compromised and they needed to make sure I had had my MRI. I tried to inform them that I had just had one done in the last couple days. They didn't listen and took me for the MRI anyway. They told Heidi to stay put in the room and I would be returned very soon. They whipped me down to the MRI room and had me scanned. I had to take out my Shackle earring for the scan and it disappeared after that. Sad.

Right after the scan they quickly returned me to my room where Heidi was waiting. They asked her if she wanted to stay or go, because they were locking all the doors and we would likely be locked in several hours. She opted to stay. They locked the doors as they left. I had a big glass window wall and they pulled a metal shade down on the outside – like those metal garage doors that shops use to close up. It was very End-of-the-world Apocalypse feeling. Heidi seemed a little nervous, but not bad. She talked, I wrote, we laughed. Alarms and loud noises and loud concerned voices continued to penetrate our fortress door. Around four or five in the morning it was all over. The hospital staff opened up my room, asked how we were. Two nurses came in and gave me a quick sponge bath. We asked what had happened and what was going on, but no one really told us anything. One nurse came in and when we asked her what had happened overnight, she mentioned a bomb threat, people with guns, or something like that, but didn't go into any detail or really explain what had happened. When we told Cindy about it the next evening I don't think she really believed us. But I don't know, my perception was off. Exciting times for Heidi's visit anyway,

What else do I remember from my time in the ICU? Let's see; visit from Heather, visit from Heidi, visit from Jim. Huge Flower Bouquet from Global Diving and Salvage – the Dive company I was working for in Kentucky (they are based out of Seattle). Huge basket of Chocolate candy bars from my cousin Jon (Jim's brother). Cindy's worried face, Cindy's smiling face. Hugs from Cindy. Lock down night. My mouth being wired shut. I don't remember having it done, just waking up one day with it already done. Lots of moaning patients and crying family members – other patients, not me or my family. We tend to cry quietly in private. I am not a moaner or a screamer, besides I was feeling No pain. Morphine drip is Awesome! Smiles.

I remember two pair of nurses that would come in every day to give me a sponge bath. Mostly they would rotate. One day it would be one pair, the next it would be the other. One pair had a medium build Blonde. She was definitely in charge and a little rough. She would throw me from side to side when she flipped me over. I felt like a piece of sausage getting flipped around by Gordon Ramsey. And when she used the sponge it felt like she was rubbing me raw (where I could feel). She also didn't seem to care what the water temperature was. Sometimes it was warm, sometimes it was cold. I referred to her has my "Neo-Nazi Nurse." She did a good job, she was just rough and super bossy.

The other pair was much more gentle and friendly. One day I remember the nice pair came in and bathed me. Later that afternoon, Neo-Nazi came in to bathe me. I informed her that I had already had my bath for the day. She didn't seem to believe me and asked several times. Finally she asked if I really hadn't had a bath, but just didn't want to get bathed by her and her partner. I explained that I really did get bathed earlier that day. She said okay and turned around in kind of a huff and left. The next time she had to take blood from me, she was a little rougher than normal. I guess I should have just let her bathe/beat me up again! She was a good nurse other than that. That's about all I can remember from the ICU.

My next memory is a Twilight Zone moment. It was kind of dark and eerie, almost saw fog around the floor. It sounded like construction was going on. There were witches cackling in the background. Three or four orderlies and a couple nurses came in one after the other telling me that I was being moved to the Special Care Unit. The told me they just had to prepare the room. More construction noise. At this point it seems like I had been moved out of my room in the ICU and was waiting in a darkened hall. Still lots of cackling, gibbering, female voices in the background. Still lots of construction noises. Someone came by and told me there weren't any rooms available so they were going to put me in a supply closet. I still can't talk at this point, thank you trach-tube.

I didn't have my white board and Purple marker. I don't remember Cindy being around. Later someone came by and told me they were putting a room together for me. More construction noises. Were they building an addition onto the Hospital for me? Were they building a room in the hall? Were they converting a waiting room? I didn't know. I closed my eyes then opened them.

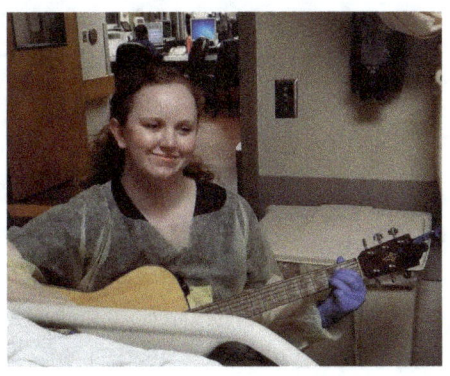

Now I am in the middle of a large white room. One wall is all windows. The floor is tiled white. There is a piano against one wall and a girl is playing it and singing. An orderly comes in and says I have too much mail coming in and they don't know what to do with it. I still don't have my Purple Marker. I feel like Harold, but lost the Purple Crayon. Still no Cindy anywhere. I am sure she was right by my side, but I must have been in some sort of weird dream state. The Twilight Zone, I'm telling you! The piano player left and a guitar player came in and started playing the guitar and singing. A group of girls were in the corner talking and giggling. I closed my eyes and slept. When I woke up I was in a small Hospital room. Cindy was sitting to my right. There was a window to my left.

The room was very small, maybe ten feet by twenty. It was long from the door to the Window and my bed was in the middle perpendicular to the length, so there was only a couple feet, maybe three, at the foot of my bed to the wall. There was an armoire in the corner by the window. Up against the window was stacked some Hospital equipment. It blocked about half the window. The hospital staff said they had no where else to store it, but it wouldn't cause us any problem. All it did was make a small room smaller and blocked off my view through the window. It wasn't very convenient for the nursing staff. This is where my memory starts to be better. I think I remember every day in the Special Care Unit. I still had a Twilight zone episode or two, but those were probably just weird dreams, or maybe times in the night when I was asleep and a nurse would come in to take blood or something. My room was right next to the Nurses' Station. That's where all the voices and giggling came from. There were a lot of student nurses working in this ward and they seemed more interested in talking with each other at the nurses' station than they did in doing their job. If Cindy pushed the help button it might take fifteen or twenty minutes before anyone responded. All the while we could hear them jibber-jabbing and giggling at the nurses' station right outside our door. Of course it depended what nurses were on shift.

The Neo-Nazi had followed me up to this ward at least to take blood and give me medications. When she was around she would respond right away. My pain started to increase a little on this ward. I figured it must be because I was getting better and sensation was returning or maybe I was not responding to the pain medications. I no longer had the Morphine drip, sadly, but had been put on Oxy instead. Cindy thinks one of the nurses was taking my pain meds and replacing them with a placebo or aspirin or something. I don't know. He was a little jittery all the time, but he did his job well. He was one of the better ones at taking my blood, and he was more attentive than some of the other nurses. I was in this ward, the Special Care Unit for two weeks.

The nurses here took care of my bowel program. They weren't happy about doing it and one time a pile of poop fell on the floor. They didn't clean it up, instead they pushed it under my bed. "Out of sight, out of mind" I guess. After a day of not cleaning it up, Cindy kept telling every nurse that came into the room about it. They all said "okay, we'll get it taken care of." but it took three days before a janitor actually came in and cleaned it up, By that time it was stuck to the floor pretty good and they had to move my bed and scrape it off the floor. Of course, the janitor was not happy about it and asked why he hadn't been notified sooner. We couldn't give him an answer, all we could do was tell him that we had been telling the nurses for three days. The Special Care Unit is also where I developed a bed sore. Right on my Sacrum, a pretty bad place to get one.

Not that any place is a good one for a bed sore, but that hindered my progress when the Physical Therapists wanted to start working with me and teaching me to get into a wheel-chair. I developed the bed sore because the nursing staff in the Special Care Unit didn't roll me from side to side at all for four or five days. It wasn't until one of the nurses pointed out the sore while doing my bowel program that anyone seemed to notice. After that the nurses were a little more attentive to my needs.

Also at this time some Physical Therapists started visiting me every day. They worked with me teaching me to sit up, sit on the edge of the bed and balance. That may seem simple, but when you don't have ANY muscle use below your sternum it is very difficult. You can't pull yourself up with stomach muscles, you can't counter balance with legs. And try to stay sitting up with out abdominal muscles. You can't do it if you have control of your muscles – you can't "pretend" to be paraplegic or quadriplegic – because your mind moves your muscles subconsciously.

For me, sitting on the edge of the bed is like having my shoulders and head precariously balanced on the top of a slab of meat. If I don't use my arms to keep myself upright my upper body will start to fall whatever direction I happen to be leaning just a little and I can't do anything about it. It's kind of like riding a unicycle and the wheel suddenly freezes up. You are going to go down, you feel it, the balance mechanism still works in my ears, so I feel I'm falling, and I see it (unless I close my eyes!) and there is nothing I can do about it if I don't have something to grab onto or catch myself with. Even then, there is a tipping point – Ha "Tipping Point!" – where you are going down no matter what, especially if you are going backwards. You don't realize how much you use your abdominal muscles until you no longer have them.

They wanted to get me into a manual wheelchair, but because of my pressure sore, I couldn't slide into the chair. We had to use a Hoyer lift. What a pain. Is this the way the rest of my life was going to go? God, I hope not. The PTs were really good though, and very happy to work with me. I saw this as an opportunity to work towards walking again, so whatever they wanted to teach me, I wanted to learn. They said I picked up the wheelchair skills pretty quickly. I couldn't do wheelies or anything but everything else was pretty simple.

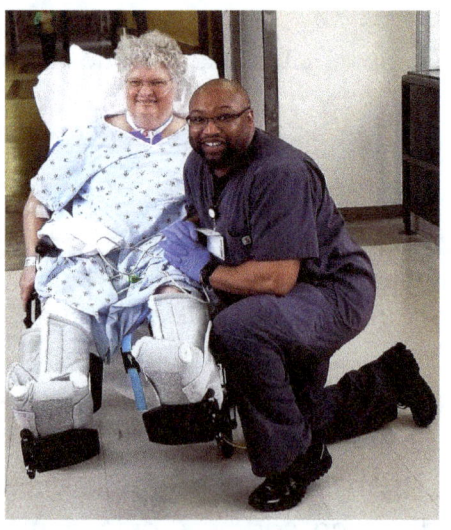

I mean anybody can push wheels and make themselves go if they have full use of their arms. My left shoulder wasn't a hundred percent, but it wasn't before either. It was worse now though. I had really limited range of motion. I had torn all the ligaments holding the ball in the socket. The doctors hadn't repaired it yet, they had already performed surgeries on my back, both my ankles, wired my upper jaw and teeth – I cracked the face bone under my nose and loosened my top row of teeth. At least I still had all my teeth in my head. Smiles. The doctors said they needed my body to heal some before they traumatized it again with another surgery, so the shoulder would just have to wait. After I was able to ingest food and drink through my mouth, I was asked what I wanted to drink. Chocolate Mile of course! Cindy found me a Chocolate Milk and it was the best Chocolate Milk I had ever had. Brent was my Physical Therapist and he was excellent. He helped me sit on the edge of the bed, taught me balancing tricks, and taught me wheelchair skills. He also taught me some arm exercises using four-pound weights. He worked with me until I moved into the next ward about a week and a half later. This Special Care Unit is also where I got the Trach-Tube removed. That is usually a slow process because I had a fairly big tube stuck in my Trachea. They would take out the big one and replace it with an incrementally smaller one. They told us I would have to go through four or five transitions and it could take a week or two. Wonderful. When they pulled the first biggest one, the hole shrunk up a little more than expected so they went down two sizes rather than just one. They checked it often and said It was healing fast and doing really well, so when they replaced it again, they asked how small I wanted to try. I told them to try the smallest one they were comfortable with. I ended up only having to do three transitions and they said that I was one of the fastest healers they had ever seen. Finally I got the trach-tube out! Yeehaw! When the last one was out and I just had a bandage over the opening, a technician came in with some kind of camera on the end of a metal snake thing. She said she was going to stick this thing up my nose and get it to go down the back of my throat and look at everything to make sure it was all okay in there. Why couldn't she just go through my mouth?! "Sorry, I have to go through your nose" she said. I think they just take joy in torturing patients. She said all looked good and asked me to make some sounds as she looked at my vocal chords. That felt weird. The Trach-Tube nurse had taught me how to talk by covering the inlet from the trach-tube so air would go through my voicebox instead of out the trach-tube. That took a little to get used to and was kind of a pain. At least now I could start talking easier and stop using my Purple marker! It took a few days before I could talk normally, but that's okay. It was way better to be able to talk. The next step was to get out of the Special Care Unit and into the Spinal Cord Injury rehabilitation unit. It was Spain Rehab at University Alabama Birmingham.

Chapter 5

It was time for me to move into Spain Rehab. Cindy got all our personal stuff gathered and ready to go. We were waiting on the nurses or orderlies to come in and move us. We had been told that we would be transferred in the early afternoon. Cindy was ready to go by ten. She really wanted to get out of the Special Care Unit because their care wasn't "Special" at all, other than it was severely lacking. We were supposed to be transferred the day before, but the Special Care Unit didn't have the paperwork ready. So I had lunch around noon and we waited. We waited. And we waited some more. We had dinner. "Oh, I don't think I'm having dinner here," I told the orderly taking my dinner order. She told me I was and that I would have dinner here or I wouldn't have it at all. Okay, what ever you say. I guess I'm having dinner here. I wonder when the Special Care Unit is going to take me down to Rehab? We had dinner. We waited. The dinner trays were taken away. We waited. We waited some more. The sun went down. We waited. Hmm, I wonder when I'm being transferred. Around ten p.m. Cindy was extremely irritated and testy. She asked when they were going to transfer me. They said they weren't finished preparing my meds for the transfer and besides orderlies from Spain Rehab were supposed to come get me. Cindy was not happy. She took off in search of the Spain Rehab unit. She could tell you better what happened, all I can tell you is second-hand news. Cindy found Spain Rehab and talked to the nursing staff there. I guess they were a little upset because they had my room ready and waiting since noon. They told Cindy that the Special Care Unit was supposed to bring me down. In the end I don't know who brought me to the Spain Rehab, I just know I got there around eleven p.m. and the only nurse on duty was attending the nurses' station and she had to check us in. I don't know what happened with my meds either. I went to sleep, I'm not sure if Cindy did.

The next morning I woke up to a whole slew of new nurses and doctors. My new doctor was great. She had a very positive demeanor. She also always had two or three interns following her around. It was the same with the nurses. There was always at least one nurse in training following around the actual nurse. I've never had so many women tending to me in my life! They were much more attentive about me taking my meds, rolling me from side to side, and caring for my comfort. Cindy had been on top of that before as much as she could be, but I am sure she didn't really know what was supposed to be done. I do know that she kept a log of everything and if she thought anything wasn't right, she let someone know. The best nurse we had was Blessing. Such a great name and she really was a Blessing. She took very good care of me AND she taught Cindy a lot about how to take care of me. She taught Cindy the correct way to care for me in every way. She went over and over all the care with Cindy until they were both comfortable that Cindy would be able to continue my care at home.

The nurses brought me a fan, to help keep me cool. They made sure I took my meds right on the dot. My pain diminished but my skin got itchy, come to find out I was slightly allergic to Oxycodone. Supposedly I had been on Oxy since I had been transferred to the Special Care Unit. I wonder why I didn't get itchy there? Also, I wonder why my pain level had increased when I moved there. I had assumed it was because they had, sadly. taken away my Morphine drip. But then why did my pain decrease after moving to the rehab unit while still being on the same meds as prescribed while I was in the Special Care Unit. Hmmm. Can anyone say drug exchange? We had no proof, but both Cindy and I are pretty sure one of the nurses had been changing out my pain meds for something less potent. I don't like pills much, so after we discovered that I must not have been on Oxy, I asked them to put me on something less addictive. We opted for Tylenol 3, then reduced it to regular Tylenol before I left the Hospital for good.

My room in the rehab unit was considerably bigger and it had a bathroom with a roll-in shower in it. There was also a ceiling mounted Hoyer lift system. That is an electric lift motor that is on tracks mounted to the ceiling so I could be moved all over the room while hanging in a sling. I kind of felt like a Christmas Ornament sometimes hanging in that sling so much! The Occupational Therapists brought in a manual wheelchair with a very high back on it. They said that would be good to support my back and they taught Cindy how to tip it back with me in it for pressure reliefs. I wheeled around in that for a day, but it was pretty hard on my left shoulder. The next day they brought in a power chair for me to use. They loaned me a Rojo cushion as well. A Rojo cushion is made up of small inflatable domes to help reduce the formation of pressure sores. You still have to move around a lot while sitting in the chair, but it is supposed to significantly reduce the risk of sores. The inflatable cushion makes it harder to slide in and out of the chair though. I didn't have to worry about that yet though. Because of the pressure sore I had on my butt, I was transferred with the Hoyer lift all the time.

Shortly after I was moved into Spain Rehab, my sister Heather visited again. My daughter, Anarachel, also made a surprise visit. She had just moved to Brooklyn, NY and didn't have much money, so my Uncle Art, my dad's  oldest brother, let her use his airline miles for a ticket from NYC to Birmingham. That was a wonderful surprise and very emotional for me. It was hard for me to keep from crying. It still brings a tear to my eye when I think about it. Every day the Physical Therapist would come in and make sure I was up, fairly early, and help the Occupational Therapist get me dressed. They were teaching me to get dressed by myself as much as I could. They gave me tools to help me do that. One was an industrial strength "grabber" compared to the ones I had seen before. I mean, the only thing I had used like that before had a grip with a trigger on the end of a long tube and a Dinosaur Head on the other end. Squeezing and releasing the trigger would open and close the dinosaur mouth. The one the OT gave me was quite a bit heavier and stronger. I used it to grip the top of socks and kind of pull them onto my feet. Then I would use it to grab the waist of pants or shorts and pull them over my feet and up until I could grab them with my hands. I could do it, but it was a LOT of work. I suppose that would get easier with time and practice. They also gave me a thing that looked like an "Invisible Dog" that you would get at Carnivals. It was used to loop my feet and move them around. It was also a lot of work, but it did help. Another tool they introduced me to were "Leg Loops." These were slid up my leg over my pants up to just above my knee. These were basically grab handles that made it easier to lift my legs up to move them around. Without the straps, I had to grab my leg underneath with my hand and lift. That took a lot more strength. Some paras hook their arm under their leg to move it around, but I wasn't flexible enough to bend down far enough to be able to do that. All that took a lot of energy and by the time I got myself half-dressed and into the chair, I was worn out. It would take me awhile before I could do that for myself. The fact of the matter is that I am not in the best physical shape and it is much easier to have Cindy help me. It gets done much faster and I am not completely worn out getting dressed and into the chair. A couple other friends visited me while I was in Rehab. One of my Dive buddies who rode a Harley, Aaron, rode up from Florida to visit. Another, my very good friend, Byron, with whom I went to Dive School. He also had lived in Helena for a while and we used to ride together quite a bit. Then he moved to Florida the year before my accident. He also rode his bike, a BMW K75S, up from Florida to visit me.

After I got dressed, the Physical Therapist, Meredith, would take me down a level in the Hospital to one of the Rehab rooms. She was an excellent teacher and I learned a lot from her. She was also kind of small – maybe five-foot-three and a hundred pounds. I was afraid I'd squish her if I fell. I never did fall on her though. She taught me well. They had all kinds of exercise equipment, padded tables, and beds. They also had a couple Hoyer lifts and several slide boards. They used a Hoyer to move me around. Meredith wanted to teach me how to use a slide board, but my butt wound prevented that. Every day she was perturbed that the Special Care Unit had allowed that sore to develop. In the rehab room, I worked with hand powered bicycle pedals, a ring toss tower, and a weight bar that I could push down on to lift weights. That was designed to work on the muscles I would use to lift myself up and down while sitting in a chair. This would make it easier for me to transfer from one chair to another, or into bed, or into a car seat. Another PT,

Randi, also worked with me teaching me how to operate the power chair. She even took me out of the Hospital to drive the chair around town on the sidewalks. She led Cindy and me to a Soup and Sandwich shop. That was the first time I had real food since I entered the Hospital. I got Cheese Soup and a Club Sandwich. It was Mahvelous! Thank you, Randi! She wouldn't let me operate it at a hundred percent because she was afraid I would crash into a wall, or so she said! Cindy agreed. Ha!

The University of Alabama at Birmingham Medical Center covered Twenty-Seven City Blocks when I was there. All the buildings were connected by Skywalks on the second level. Cindy went on a "coffee run" every morning down to a Star-buck's located in the restaurant area of the complex. She fig-ured it was about a mile and quarter there and back, so she got her exercise everyday that way. The maze of Skywalks gave me plenty of room to practice driving my power chair. On the low setting it would only go about two-and-a-half miles per hour.

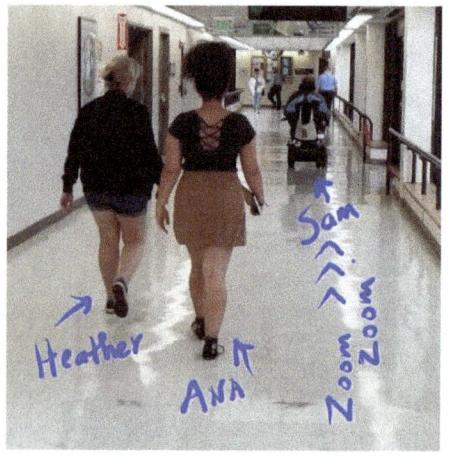

I figured out how to put it in High Power Mode and then it would go about six miles per hour. I had fun running fast and far away from Heather, Anarachel, and Cindy. Ha ha!

Other things the Physical Therapists would work with me on was rolling from side to side, being able to sit up on the side of the bed by myself, balancing myself while sitting up on the edge of a bed or table. Meredith and Randi were very good and positive about what they were doing. They had a standing frame there that I wanted to get into really badly. I wanted to be able to stand and look at people eye to eye. Even though I had only been paralyzed a few weeks by this time, I was really tired of having to look up all the time to talk to people and see their faces. It is really demoralizing to be forced into a wheelchair when you have never been in one before. Especially for me at my age, I was Fifty-Seven when I had my accident. This was a whole new ball game and I wasn't sure I wanted to play. They wouldn't put me in the standing frame. They said I had to do quite a bit of work before I would be ready to try out one of those. That sucked. I was searching all the info I could on the internet about getting to walk again – from surgeries implanting electrodes in the back to jump the damaged area of the spine, Stem Cell injections to the damaged area, genetically modified protein injections to the damaged area, to Robot Pants. Robot Pants started out as kind of a joke between Cindy and me (you know Wallace and Gromit) and an engineer friend of mine, Kirk. But I looked into it and there were actually several companies that made actual Robot Pants – not actual pants, but more like the strap on Exoskeleton stuff you see in Sci-Fi movies. Being able to stand was the first step in getting into a pair of Robot Pants. I contacted several companies but, unfortunately, my injury was too severe for me to use the existing exoskeletons.

Cindy had started a new page on my website to keep all my friends and riding buddies informed of my progress. The first month I was in the hospital I was in no shape to update my site and I had become incognito on the internet. Before my accident I visited a couple of Indian Motorcycle Forums fairly regularly and I posted on my website often. After my accident, I disappeared. Many people must have contacted Cindy to find out what the deal was. She decided to use my website to let people know and also gave them a platform on which they could let me know what they were up to or wish me well. That was really uplifting for me. I still can hardly believe how much effort Cindy put in on my behalf. She let people know when it would be a good time for visits. Bernard had contacted Cindy about setting up a day to visit and to my great surprise, they had set a day where three of my Indian Motorcycle friends would visit me. That visit took place close to the time I would check out of the Hospital. When I saw Doug and Jason, I couldn't help myself – I Blubbered like a Baby. I was not conscious of why I broke down in tears. I just looked at them and started crying. The same thing happened to me when my friends Aaron and Byron visited.

Thinking back on it, it may have been the subconscious realization that I wouldn't ever be riding with them again. Now I am not sure that will be true. I am looking into several different ways of getting back into Motorcycle riding whether it be a Sidecar Rig, Spyder type thing or some other type of rig. I look at the Trikes and I think "more power to you, and I'm glad you're on the road, but Trikes are just not for me. I apologize to Trike riders; I don't think any less of you for riding them. I just don't like them. I've seen some pretty cool trikes and I've driven a few – mostly VW powered ones and a couple Harley Trikes – they're just not for me. And even though, Spyders and other rigs with two wheels in front and one in the rear have three wheels, they are not Trikes. I do not know what they are called, but they are not Trikes. I like them more than Trikes. It has a LOT to do with stability. Remember the Three-wheelers from the seventies and eighties? They were outlawed for a reason – too many people getting hurt and killed on them. They are inherently unstable at speed. Four-wheelers are a close second in my opinion. They look stable, and subconsciously they seem more stable, but a dirt bike is a much safer ride, especially on uneven and hilly terrain. Sidecars aren't great on traversing hills sideways either, but they are more stable than Trikes. Okay, enough of that!

Back to the Occupational Therapists. They got me into a Shower Chair and gave me my first shower in over a month. Boy did that feel good. It was weird taking a shower sitting down though, not that I could do anything about it. Plus, I couldn't reach my back or lean forward by myself and wash my back with a sponge or brush on a stick. I couldn't reach my butt hole and I couldn't reach below my knees. My back was still pretty stiff and my left arm was not much help. I have never been like a "Manly Man" you know like when women say "Oh, you're such a Man!" in disgust. But I am a Male and proud of it. So, this shower in a chair thing was a little emasculating. Just another reason added on to the pile of reasons that made me doubt if it is all worth it. It would be so much easier to just lie down and stop breathing. The thing is you can't do that. IF you can hold your breath long enough to pass out, and that's a pretty big "IF," your body will automatically start breathing again and you wake up, maybe with a slight headache. Don't ask me how I know. Anyway, all the nurses, PTs, OTs, and family bent over backwards to support me and teach me how to live a little more independently. I appreciated all their input and support and tried to stay positive for them. Especially for Cindy. She is so awesome, I wanted to try to keep her happy.

My upper jaw was still wired. Cindy had been trying for a couple weeks to get that specialist in to remove the wiring in my mouth. It wasn't real comfortable and my gums were starting to grow around the wires. The specialist's office would make an appointment, then cancel it. That happened three or four times. About now I had been in the UAB Hospital seven weeks – forty-nine days. The Hospital administrators had decided it was about time I checked out of the Hospital, they were not supportive of me being in Spain Rehab. I don't know why, maybe my insurance company was starting to hem and haw about the length of my stay, I don't know. They sent people down with paperwork to start the checkout process and we were told I would be checked out in a week or so.

Cindy was more than ready to get us back home to Montana anyway. She missed her cats, Spook and Boo, and I am sure they missed her too. The jaw specialist made an appointment for six days away and guaranteed he would be there to remove the wires from my upper jaw. That was scheduled for just a day before I would be checking out. Cindy talked to our insurance representative, who actually worked for the Diver's Union of which I was a member. They secured a Medical flight for me that would fly me directly from Birmingham to Helena. This kind of took on a life of its own and before we knew it, I was being checked out. They ended up checking us out four days early, so I never got the wires removed from my Jaw. I had that done in Helena after I got home. The PTs and OTs hadn't really finished with me yet. Well, Montana bound we were!

Chapter 6

I know we got here kind of abruptly, but that's how it felt leaving the UAB Hospital. We weren't quite ready and neither was the staff. The flight crew was very nice and the flight was very comfortable. They had a "Hyperbaric Blanket" to cover me with which was fun, because of my diving career. A hyperbaric blanket isn't really anything special, it's just verified one hundred percent cotton and stamped with the words "Hyperbaric Use Only" so it doesn't get mixed up with other blankets on a dive job.

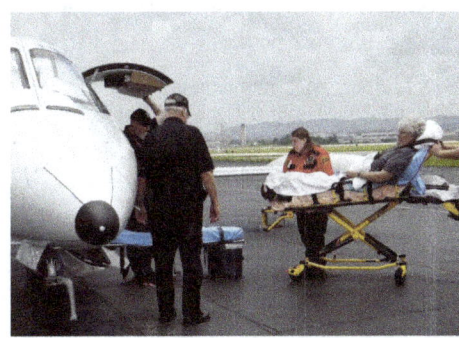 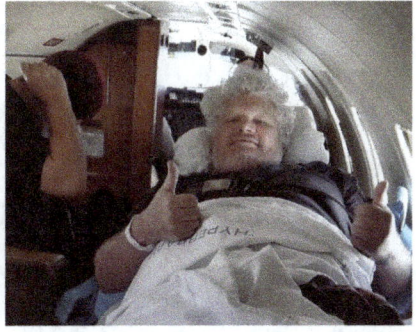

It has to be one hundred percent cotton so it doesn't cause any sparks from static electricity. Sparks in a pressurized hyperbaric chamber will be catastrophic. Anyway, it was nice to be wrapped in a dive blanket. We weren't allowed, by some policy – I don't know whose, to transfer directly from the Hospital to our home if a Medical Flight was used. I had to check into a care facility in Helena. Cindy and the insurance company had that all set up before we took off. Our flight took a little longer than expected due to weather, so we arrived at the care center about fifteen minutes late. The senior staff and on-site administrators made a HUGE deal about us being late. They didn't give me my meds for the night, because I was late and they informed us that they couldn't just reschedule my meds without a doctor's permission, so I didn't get any meds until the next morning. Needless to say, I didn't sleep well that night due to the pain. The administrator came in with a pile of papers for me to sign. I still wasn't really all there. She told me the papers were just the standard stuff and I didn't need to read through them. I almost signed a DNR – Do Not Resuscitate form – but Cindy caught me just in time. She was adamant about going through all the paperwork before any-thing was signed. To say the least, Cindy and the administrator did not get off to a good start.

The senior staff was really nasty too. There were three senior nurses that ran the place and they were crotchety old ladies. They acted like they knew everything and no one else knew anything. They were really condescending to the younger staff. My meds were distributed by the nursing staff. I couldn't keep my meds in my room, even though Cindy was there with me almost all the time. One time I didn't get my meds on time so one of the younger nurses brought me my medication and just as she gave it to me, the senior nurse burst into my room screaming "What are you doing?! You can't do that! Give me those and get out of here! Go clean up room 23!" The younger nurse tried to explain that she was just trying to help, but the senior nurse just kept berating her. I felt really bad for the younger nurse. The senior nurse finally gave me my meds and left. I felt like I was in an episode of American Horror Story. Where was Nurse Ratched?

My upper jaw was still wired, so I was still under direction to eat only soft foods. We were informed that this care center couldn't prepare special meals just for me. In order for them to meet my doctor's orders for soft food only, they informed me that all my meals would be run through a blender before being served to me. Ever had blended Enchiladas? How about a blended Bacon Cheeseburger. It wasn't that different from the blended Chili-Mac I had for the previous meal. Breakfasts were the only semi-normal meals I had because I could have fruit-flavored yogurt, or oatmeal. Oh, well, at least I was being fed.

I had several issues with my bed also. First off it was too small. When I lay flat, my head would touch the Headboard and my feet would touch the Footboard. When I was sitting up, my feet were pressed up against the Footboard. It was also kind of narrow. I couldn't roll from side to side without being pulled one way or another. There were no side rails either. I would use the side rails to pull myself onto one side or the other for pressure reliefs and bathroom activities. I was informed that it was illegal for the bed to have side rails mounted. I didn't understand that, because all my hospital beds had them. Well, no matter it was against the law and you're not gettin' 'em No way, No how! Okay, Okay, sheesh. How about a bigger bed, please? "We don't have any bigger beds" they informed me. Hmmm. Okay. I'm not that big of a person, what do they do if somebody of some real size comes in? I wondered. A couple days later I was told that if I really needed a bigger bed, they could get one from Missoula but it would take at least three or four days to get here. That's funny, Missoula is only two hours away from Helena. Cindy was anxious to get me out of there as soon as possible and I wanted to leave as soon as I could also. The place was really depressing. There were two younger nurses – mid to late twenties – who were nice and did their jobs well. They actually seemed to care for the patients, but they were constantly being tormented by the senior staff. I spent seven days there. I had to get the okay from a doctor to leave. The care center had an accessible van, but it never seemed to be operational. Cindy had to hire an ambulance to get me to my doctor's appointment, even though the law states that the care centers are obligated to get their residents to their doctor's appointments. I think they wanted me to stay, because I had good insurance at the time.

I got the okay from the doctor to leave. When I got back to the care center, we tried to schedule a leave date, but now they said I had to have my own personal wheelchair before I left. We had one on order from Spectrum Medical, but it wouldn't be ready for a while and supposedly Spectrum didn't have any loaners. Cindy was getting pissed. She went down to the local Goodwill and rented one for three months. When she brought it to the care center, Spectrum informed us that they had one we could use until my special ordered one showed up. Were they in cahoots with the care center? I do not know. Sometimes it is not great to have really good insurance. Also going through all this, I see why health insurance is so expensive. All these health providers and medical equipment providers are thieves. It's unbelievable what they charge the insurance companies. Most recently, we needed a new Low-Loss Air Mattress because the air pump on mine failed. We called Spectrum (they've recently changed their name) and they informed us that we couldn't repair or replace just the air pump because the company no longer manufactured that pump. We would have to purchase a complete mattress/pump combo unit. Cindy told them that would be okay. They said their technician would bring one down the next day. We had thought they were treating us fairly well. Their technician brought it and put it on my bed. Cindy asked how much it would be and he answered it would be about thirty-four hundred dollars. Cindy asked if we could bill insurance. He didn't know, he did say

Medicare probably would not cover it, but if we rent-to-owned it we could probably run it through insurance and it wouldn't cost us any more either way.

Cindy agreed to that and gave him a check for the first month's rent. When Cindy figured we were getting close to paying it off, she called and asked for a record of payments and a bill for the final payment. She had been asking for a paper trail on the mattress since we got it, but they kept putting her off. Finally, she got a little nasty with them and they told her that, no, the price wasn't necessarily thirty-four hundred dollars. They informed Cindy that the insurance companies had given them a price limit of ten thousand dollars for Low-Loss air mattresses. Ten Thousand Dollars!! Spectrum quoted Cindy a cost of $9,794.00 usd!! Are You Kidding me! Cindy told them we were paying on our own, out of pocket, because Medicare wouldn't cover it due to the fact that I didn't have an active wound. Medicare doesn't pay for preventative medical supplies. The people at Spectrum didn't care, they had indicated that they were allowed to charge the insurance companies ten thousand dollars, so that is what they were going to charge us. Are you Kidding me!?! We were quoted thirty-four hundred and that is all Cindy was going to pay, or they could come and take this mattress right back. Then Cindy went on line. She found the EXACT same mattress on line for sale at the MSRP of twenty-four ninety-five. Yes, that is correct; two thousand, four hundred, and ninety-five dollars.

On top of that, the internet site showed, that mattress was on sale at this time for eighteen ninety-five – almost a Third Less than the MSRP. Screw Spectrum. Cindy was really pissed. She forwarded the internet site to Spectrum to show them she knew what they were up to. Finally, they agreed to sell it to her for the MSRP of twenty-four ninety-five. Cindy made the final payment to them and we are not dealing with them anymore. This kind of business has to stop. I'm a capitalist, I mean that is what makes the world go around, for human society anyway, but business people need to have some sort of conscience. Where's Jiminy Cricket when you need him? This greed is what is destroying the world as we know it, it's not Capitalism, it is Greed.

Anyway, after Cindy got the wheelchair situation straightened out, we got an exit date from the care center. They informed us that they still didn't have a working accessible van. That's okay, Cindy was prepared to rent an ambulance if necessary and we had heard that Helena Transit had accessible vans and we could schedule a pickup with them. "Oh no, you don't need to contact them, our van is working now," the administrator told Cindy. "We will schedule with our driver to take you home at one p.m. the next day." Yay, I was getting out of this place. I slept okay that night. Cindy got up fairly early and made sure we were all packed up and I was ready to go. The young nurses and Cindy got me into my loaner chair and we were ready to go about noon. We went on out to the front to meet the van.

Just after we got out front, the care center van pulled up and we thought "alright something is going right for once." It was about ten to one, so the van was right on time. The driver, an older female, turned off the van, got out and asked if we were the people needing the ride. We told her we were. She said "Fine, you might want to wait inside the building though because my lunch hour is just starting. I will load you up at two." Ach Du Lieber Gott!!! You have GOT to be kidding me. It is just one thing after another with these people. Am I in another episode of Twilight Zone? Is this some new form of Horror Show?! Please, just let me leave! We did get loaded up at two and she did take us home. She didn't know the way, so Cindy sat up front and guided her. We ran over a couple curbs and ran through at least one Red Light. She also exceeded the speed limit most of the way. Boy will I be glad to be out of these people's grasp. We finally made it home. Whew.

Chapter 7

Oh, it was so nice to see my home. There was a ramp covering the steps to my back porch. Our good friend, Jim, had volunteered his own time and materials to put that ramp in for us and made sure it would be completed and ready to use before we got home. Thank You Jim! I drove my powerchair up the ramp and into the Dining Room through the back door, which has now become our "Front Door" or at least the door we use all the time. We rarely open the Front doors anymore. Cindy had a hospital bed set up for me in the Dining room. Both the Dining Room and my Library had been emptied of its furniture to make room for me. This was sad for me, I really liked the way we had been furnishing it, trying to keep with the Victorian theme. Life, you never know what cards you are going to be dealt. Joker's Wild, and the Big Dealer in the Sky is the Joker! Cindy had all the furniture removed so we could move stuff in that would make it better for me and easier for her to take care of me. I didn't need as many clothes, but I needed lots of other supplies, both medical and hygiene stuff, you know, like Diapers. I have to wear Diapers again. Could be emasculating, but at this point, I just don't care anymore. Call me baby Huey! I'd rather have a beer than a Pacifier though! Irish Death or Guinness please! Heather likes to drink Irish Car Bombs with me. I lived in the Dining Room for a little over a month while we got the Library all set up for me. My friends, Tom and Bridget, bought me a large TV for my room so Cindy wouldn't have to move our other TV downstairs. Tom said I needed something to watch Indian cream Harley in the dirt Flat Track Races. You know it, Tom! Indian is cleaning up with that new FTR. I'd Love to ride one of those.

Finally, I got moved into the Library. Two bookshelves had been moved out, but the two built-in book cases were still full of my books. It helped to make me feel a little more at home. The Big Screen TV was situated at the foot of my bed, a rolling nightstand was placed to my right, so I could set my phone, water, pills and other stuff I wanted to keep handy on it. Life was heading towards a new normal. Cindy did everything she could to make things better for me.

Now that things were calming down for me, I had more time to think about my situation and my future. I didn't have nurses coming in poking me and prodding me every hour. I didn't have Physical Therapists get me up every day to work on my body. I didn't have orderlies coming into my room several times a day to feed me, take away dirty dishes, or clean. Now it was all up to Cindy and she had her real job, plus our two cats to take care of, not to mention our large house and yard that needed cleaning and maintaining. Oh Joy! I couldn't do much to help out either, at least not anywhere near the way I used to.

Insurance helped pay for a Physical Therapist to come in for thirty visits the first year. That is not even once a week. The doctors had said I should meet with one at least twice a week. After we exhausted the in-house visits, insurance paid for six months of Physical Therapy at a rehabilitation center. We went twice a week. It was kind of a pain, but at least I got out of the house once in a while, I suppose. Covid hit about the time my insurance ran out, so we stopped going to that. Then we hired a caregiver from a local business that supplies caregivers to people who need them. They are not certified nor are they really trained to care for someone like me. Luckily, they sent a girl, Anna, who was a pre-Med student at Carrol College. She had worked a little with a massage therapist and had worked a little with a physical therapist so she had a pretty good handle on how to help me. She came in twice a week to stretch me and help me with upper body exercises. She was fantastic. She worked with us for two-and-a-half years. She graduated in spring 2022 and, sadly, has moved on.

Anyway, Cindy was doing everything for me now, mostly by herself. With her job, taking care of the cats, taking care of the house, taking care of life, she ended up leaving me to my own devices for quite a lot of the time. She usually checked in at the very least every couple hours if she had to leave the house. When she was in the house, she would check on me every half hour at least, just poke her head in and see if I was doing okay. I had my phone right next to me all the time and she carried her phone with her, so I could call her whenever I needed. She got a dinger thing that was basically an electronic bell. It had a button I could push and it would ding on a receiver elsewhere in the house so Cindy could hear it if she was out of shouting distance. That worked pretty well. She had a dinger by her bed so I could ding her in the middle of the night if I needed something.

What this all meant was that I had a lot of time to myself. I watched a lot of TV, I read some, I messed around on the computer. I wrote a little on my computer. Cindy got puzzles for me, my friend, Byron, gave me a huge book of Sudoku puzzles. I checked Facebook. And I contemplated my situation a Lot. I mean a LOT. I didn't really feel sorry for myself, but I did ask myself "Why?" all the time. I asked "Why me? Why not some-one else who deserved it more? Why not some Evil person? I wasn't Evil, was I?" I asked myself if maybe I deserved this. But then why me, again? I mean if I deserved it, surely other people deserved it more. The more I thought about it the more I thought "Why NOT me?" I mean, nobody really deserves this kind of thing. It just happens. It happens to all kinds of people in all kinds of places. I went into a fairly dark place. I mean I wasn't happy to be alive.

I felt like I lost everything. I didn't, I still had Cindy. Her life was completely messed up now though. My accident and current condition completely changed her situation. I couldn't work in the Dive industry anymore. I wouldn't be bringing in any more money. I couldn't work on the house – it still needs a lot of stuff done to it. I couldn't work in the yard – that is an ongoing and never-ending job. I couldn't ride my bikes. I couldn't drive. I guess it was a good thing I had to sell my Convertible Bug back to VW because of its Diesel engine. I hated my life and my situation. I hated days with Blue Skies because I couldn't ride anymore. I hated the sound of Motorcycles going by. That just reminded me of what I was missing. I hated seeing Motorcycles on the road when Cindy took me places in our van. I hated waking up to Fresh Snow in the morning with a Blue, Blue Sky. That used to be one of my favorite kind of days to wake up because I would run out to the garage, start up my Ural and go make tracks in the fresh snow. I didn't care how cold it was, It was great to be riding a Sidecar in the fresh snow on a cold, sunny morning. Now I hated fresh snow on a cold, sunny morning.

Every morning I would wake up disappointed that I hadn't passed away during the night. What was I doing still alive? I was a useless body, wasting natural resources. Wasting lots and lots of natural resources, plus adding to the garbage problem. I mean look at all the plastic, rubber, and paper trash generated by taking care of me: Diapers, Rubber or Nitrile Gloves, Babywipes, Paper Towels, Lotions in Plastic Bottles, Creams in Plastic containers or metal tubes, Absorbent Cloths so my bed wouldn't get soiled, not to mention the Cardboard Boxes all my supplies came in. $#!T, I could fill a Landfill all by myself now.

I couldn't do anything on my own either, so not only messing up my life, I messed up someone else's too. Then you have all the positive people, the Shiny, Happy People. They tell you things like "You're so Lucky to be alive!" or "You can still do so much." or "God has a plan for you." F@%k that god. Take that god and stuff him up where the Sun don't Shine Mother F@%ker. Recently I went to a camp for people with Spinal Cord Injuries, Empower SCI, and met a therapist there, Toni, who talked about "Toxic Positivity." That's Exactly what it is. People think they are being positive and uplifting, but all you really want to do is Smash them in their Face and tell them to Stuff it! They don't know what I'm going through. They don't know what I am dealing with on a daily basis. Screw them, it just pisses me off and makes me hate my situation even more. If you haven't been here, you have ZERO idea what it's like.

You can play around in a wheelchair, you can walk with a walker or a cane, but if your body isn't damaged you have NO idea what it's like. Can you poop by yourself? Or do you need someone to stick their finger up your Butt everyday to make you poop? Can you Pee by yourself? Or do you have to have a tube stuck up your penis several times a day. Or maybe you have a colostomy bag that has to be emptied all the time, and if the tube gets kinked your bladder won't empty and you go into Autonomic Dysreflexia, which could send you to the Hospital. If you don't, you have NO idea of what I go through every day. AD can be caused by all kinds of things too: wrinkles in bed sheets, shoes too tight, body in a bad position, something poking into a part of my body I can't feel. Can you take a shower by yourself? Can you wash your own Butthole? If you can, you don't know what I go through. I'm not the only one, and I don't even have it as bad as others. At least I can brush my own teeth, feed myself, write with a pencil or pen. See I am lucky enough to have nearly full use of my upper body.

I think I have my full mental capabilities, but I might be wrong on that point. I did hit my head pretty hard. I was wearing my Nolan Full Face Modular Helmet, but it broke in the accident, my glasses popped off my face and a lens popped out of those, also broke my upper mandible and loosened all my upper front teeth. It's a good thing I was wearing my Helmet. Or was it? Cindy is happy I was. I stay alive for her, and for my dad, and for my kids, and my sister Heather. If it wasn't for them, I would have given up the ghost a Long time ago. It also gave me time to consider and reconsider what had happened to make me crash.

I wanted photos of my Bike. I wish I'd had a video of the actual accident. It would be great if a stress analysis engineer could look at my bike and see if something was wrong with the bike, more to the point, the Steering Head and Neck.

Look at the photos and you'll see what I'm getting at. See how the Neck split right in half? I know I hit that Concrete Highway divider head on at close to Sixty-five mph – that's about what I had the Cruise Control set at. Why it wouldn't shut off I don't know. Front Tire hit first, obviously. The Bike flipped over it and ended up in three pieces; the Front Fork section with Half the Steering Head/Neck assembly, the Fuel Tank completely separated from the Frame, and the rest of the Bike. The Front Fork part was still connected to the rest of the bike by the Wiring Harness, which I thought was rather strange. The wiring harness was cut later to make it easier to move the pieces around.

Why, oh Why did my bike go into the Tank Slap? I pondered and pondered this. I still ponder it. Was the neck stretched or stress-cracked from having a Sidecar mounted to the Bike? If so, why aren't all the other Indians with Sidecars mounted having issues? Did the Asphalt Snakes have something to do with it? Did I get slippery, sticky mud in my tires from visiting the Haunted Chicken House and that caused an issue? Were my steering head bearings loose? When I originally had the Sidecar put on by Hannigan, they told me that my Steering Head Bearings were a little loose and they tightened them up for me as part of mounting the sidecar. Was there something slippery in the road I hadn't noticed? Was it a combination of these things? I didn't know, and I still don't know. All I know is that my Bike is totaled, I am paralyzed and feel like I am totaled, but my life is not over. That's it. That's All I know. Now you know what the HELL happened to me and I can finally talk about it. That is one chapter in my life and, even though I hadn't been for the past four years, I am now looking forward to the next chapter of my life, thanks to the people of Empower SCI for getting me where I am now. That experience liberated me and freed me from some of the demons that I developed after my accident. I hope my future still involves Motorcycles and Sidecars. I am sure it will. Happy riding! Keep the Shiny side up and the rubber side down if you can help it.

Cindy and sam

Pop and sam

Wolf Creek Offroad Sidecar Racing Team

Cindy and sam

Buffalo Helmet

Bryan, Doug, Johnny, and sam

sam ready to leave home

Cindy in the Sidecar

sam visited Larry in Nebraska on his way South

Horseshoe Bend National Military Park

Copper Frog

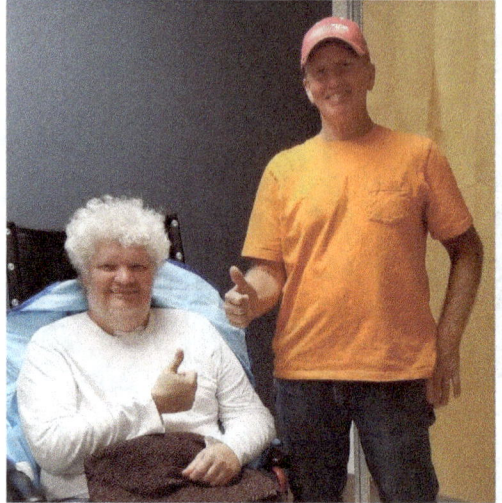

sam and Byron in UAB

Coming up Roses for Uncle Art

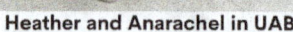

Heather and Anarachel in UAB

In the Wind

In the Snow

Cindy's Favorite Tattoo

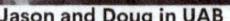

Jason and Doug in UAB

Hallowe'en

sam and cousin Jim

Pete

sam and A.W

Larry and sam

The Love of sam's Life, Cindy

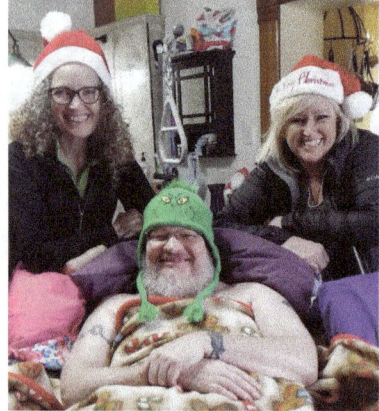
Heidi, sam, and Heather

Sammy, sam, and Anarachel

Connie, Jeff, sam, and Cindy

Greg, Cindy, sam, and Jim

Haley, Donna, and JoAnn

Tom and Bridget

Lauren, RyanB, and Mike

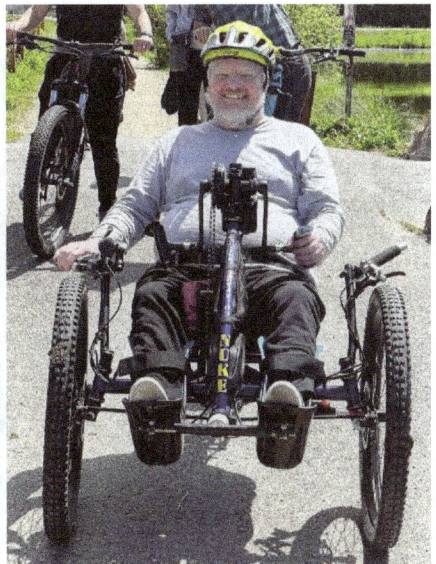

sam on tricycle

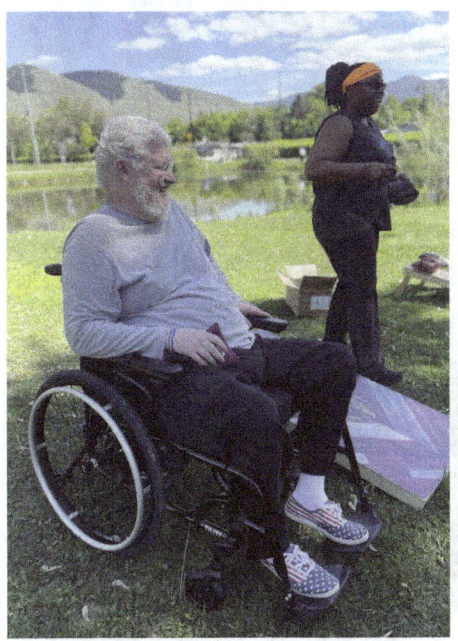

Motor-Powered Trike

sam and Mo watching other team toss

Mo watches sam make a toss

Sam, Mike, Andrew, Maggie

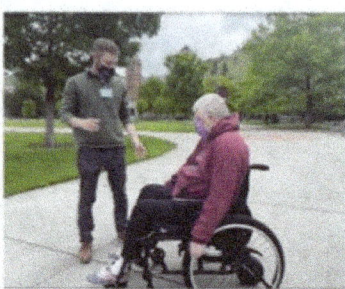

Troy and Sam

Ryan B and Liz

Ryan B

Ryan B and Bre

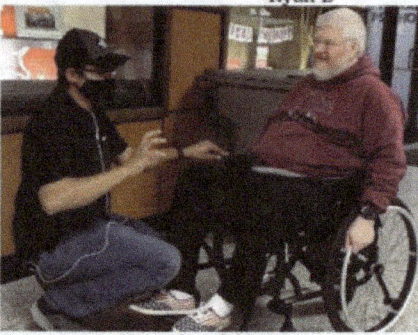

Lionel and Sam

Bodhi

Sam and Heather

Chalynne, Bre, Meaghan, and Sammi

LoriC, Shelby, and Phoebe

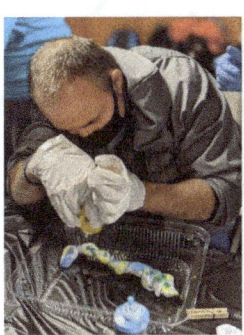

Ken is really
getting into it!

Ken, Jimmy, Kelly, and RyanO

Cat got more Dye on her
hands than on her sox!

RyanB, Tom, and Girls

Section Two

Empower Camp 2022

Four Years After My Accident

My Experience with Empower SCI

Chapter 8

Preparing to Go

Here is where my Empower SCI story starts. It was such an Incredible experience it is hard to describe. I cannot say enough about how much this week with the Empower group has affected my life. However, it wasn't all candy and roses for me right off the bat. I had a Catastrophic Motorcycle Accident on June 3rd, 2018. I was riding my Motorcycle on a small Highway in Central Alabama heading North to Kentucky. I spent about two months in the UAB hospital – University of Alabama Birmingham. That was an incredible place – twenty-seven City Blocks Huge! It is a training hospital which was really good for us because they taught Cindy how to take care of me. We had no idea how important that would be once we got back home to Helena, Montana. Also, if I hadn't been sent there, I probably would have died which, when I woke up after a few weeks. I wondered why I hadn't. We got back to Helena the last week of July and I had to be checked into a care facility. It was Horrible. The senior staff were rude, mean, and condescending. The building itself looked like it hadn't been updated since the early Sixties. I kept expecting Nurse Ratched to show up. Seriously, the place was right out of a season of American Horror Story. The walls were even painted that gross dark green on the bottom half with a lighter green on the top half. The first time I went in for a shower they put me in some contraption made out of PVC tubing with cheapo plastic wheels (they didn't have proper shower chairs). When we got to the shower there was a huge pile of Poop right in the middle of the shower floor. When Cindy alerted the staff about it, nobody wanted to clean it up. In fact, the staff refused to clean it up, so Cindy did it just so she could give me a shower. The staff refused to help Cindy at all. I thought I was in Hell and wondered if this is what the rest of my life was going to be like. Cindy got me out of there as soon as she could, still took over a week though. We finally got home. Cindy's good friend, Jim, had built a ramp up to our back door so I could get in our house. That was the best gift I had ever received. Now we're home, but our home was not set up at all for someone in my new condition. Some of Cindy's friends had cleaned out our Library. We had decided to turn that into my Bedroom since I couldn't get to our bedroom on the 2nd floor. Our bathroom on the second floor wasn't accessible for me anyway. I was set up in our Dining room right off the bat. Super inconvenient for Cindy and any visitors to the house. I was really feeling like a burden on everybody. What the Hell was I even still doing here? Cindy was working her butt off taking care of me. It was expensive keeping me stocked up with all the equipment and supplies I needed. Cindy had to cut down on her hours from her real job. We weren't getting any help from any places in Helena and, truthfully, we didn't know what help was available. Help was Not very easy to find either. We checked in with MILP (Montana Independent Living Project) here in Helena and they were not much help at all. The Hospital had no idea what was available and the staff were not helpful at all either. In fact, the Wound Care Center told us they couldn't accommodate me and we would have to go to Great Falls, 2 hours away, for Wound Care. You have GOT to be kidding me! Our hospital here had, and has, only 1, yes that's right ONE, Hoyer lift for the whole Hospital, Emergency Room and all! Despicable. Thankfully we have a good friend who helps build custom homes and he helped make the Library more useful for Cindy and me. At least now I could live like a half-way decent Human Being. I still felt like half a man, but at least my living conditions were better and the love of my life was still by my side. If she left, there would really be no point for me to continue. She spent hours and hours a day on the phone and on the internet trying to find any kind of resources or assistance. Montana just does not have much available. One of the Physical Therapists that I had been working with in Helena had graduated from the U of M PT program. He told us we should schedule a session with them if we could. Cindy got that done. In August of 2019 we went to Missoula and had a session with them. We met with Molly and Troy. They hooked me up to a computer to read something from my legs. I didn't really know what they were doing. I was thinking if this is going to get me walking again, I will do whatever they ask. Next, they hooked me up to a Bicycle pedal machine and put electrodes on my legs and my chest, I think. The computer of the machine would crank the pedals flexing my legs. At the same time it would send electrical impulses to my leg muscles to make them actually operate the pedaling. It was an interesting machine; we would have liked to have one at home. Molly told Cindy about some woman named Anita who was connected to some group from New York that worked with people who had Spinal Cord Injuries. Cindy talked to Anita. Anita told her about Empower. Cindy got excited about that and started researching it and telling me about it. Yeah, yeah, that's all I need; another group of people telling me I'm So lucky and should be thankful to be alive. Cut the crap, I've heard it enough. I was tired of people telling me how lucky I was, tired of them giving me inspirational books, tired of them telling me about all these people who have moved on and were doing amazing things. Screw that and leave me be. My favorite movie now was Me Before You. My dad was in his mid-80s and I couldn't die before he did. I couldn't break his heart like that, my accident was hard enough on him. I figured I'd wait around until after he was gone, then I could go. You may think that is selfish, but if you haven't been where I've been, you have no idea what I am going through. I look at all the medical supplies and all the day to day supplies needed to take care of me and think "that is not very Green, I am a waste of natural resources." I would look at all the energy and time and equipment needed to take care of me and think to myself "what a waste." Anyway, Cindy got me signed up for the Empower 2020 week in Montana. I agreed to go and be a good sport about it. Cindy was putting so much effort into it, that was the least I could do. Then, as everybody knows, COVID19 happened. It messed everything up. Not for me, my life didn't change much, but the 2020 Empower became a virtual experience. Yeah, I already don't like Zoom and the virtual thing just isn't me. I like Real experiences that I can touch, smell, and taste. We decided not to participate in the virtual experience. Not much changed in my life. I was watching a lot of TV, reading a little, writing a little. I just didn't have the drive to do much anymore. I was just waiting for my dad to kick his bucket so I could kick mine shortly thereafter. Of course, I never said that to anyone. When I talked to my dad, which is like once a week I tried to stay positive and keep him positive. I always told him I was doing well. I'd tell him to keep exercising and eating right. I told him any day above ground was a good one. Although I wasn't sure I believed that anymore. He'd tell me to take care of myself and I'd respond that I would if he took care of himself. He and his wife try to visit a few times a year. It was hard for me to travel and really, I had lost interest in it. Some friends would come around, but most of them have kind of faded away. 2021 came and went without an Empower program in Montana, and really, I didn't even think about it. In March 2022 Sue Ostertag contacted Cindy and told her to touch base with Anita Santasier with Empower. Cindy did. Then she asked me if I was interested in going to the U of M for a week in June for the Empower thing. Not really, I thought, but told Cindy to do whatever she thought was best. Cindy seemed really excited about the program. I was not, but if it would make Cindy happy, I would do it. She got all the paperwork done, scheduled our life around that and was looking forward to getting me signed up and accepted. I was kind of hoping they wouldn't have room for me. Then I was accepted. Cindy paid the fee. I guess I was going. Cindy told me I could back out if I really wanted. I told her I would give it a go. We had a few things come up for the week of June 12th to the 18th, a wedding reception, proposed visits from family, etc. We told them all that I had other plans and would be out of town that week. Cindy started packing for me at least a week before I had to leave. She enlisted some help to get our van loaded on the Saturday before. We got up early for us on Sunday and she loaded me into our van. "Here we go" I thought, "No backing out now."

Chapter 9

The Trip to Missoula

I rolled up into our van and Cindy strapped me down. She closed the rear door, climbed in the driver's seat and started the van. Here we go I thought. I had no idea what to expect and figured Cindy has gotten me this far I might as well jump in with both feet. That is IF I could jump! I guess I would just Roll with it and do everything they offered. Go big or Go home, right? The ride wasn't bad. I can't see much out of the windows because of the height of my power chair in the back of the van, so I just put my phone on Airplane Mode and played some games – mostly Bird Sort Color – it's a puzzle type game. I like games to keep my mind sharp; word games, Sudoku, Tetris, stuff like that. Cindy stopped in Drummond for a snack and leg stretch. I stayed in the van. A couple on a Motorcycle pulled up beside us and parked. I looked at the bike, it was a smaller Honda Adventure Bike and it was plated in Brasil. They had a small Brasilian flag flying from their luggage. We asked where they were from and they said Curitiba, Brasil. They had ridden their Bike all the way from there to the USA. They flew their Bike over the Darien Gap between Columbia and Panama. They were heading to Seattle. I remember passing them before we pulled into Drummond. The trip they were making was the reverse of one I had always wanted to do. Of course, I wanted to DRIVE through the Darien Gap and I wanted to do that on my Russian Sidecar Rig. No sidecar rig has ever made that voyage and only around a hundred motorcycles have done it. Just a handful of cars and trucks have successfully made the trek. It was a good omen, I think, to see them on our way to the Empower week in Missoula. The rest of the trip went smoothly and passed by fairly quickly. We arrived at the U of M Campus and didn't see any wheelchairs or people. Lots of Construction going on though. Cindy pulled into the parking lot by the security building and found out where we needed to go. She pulled up in front of Pantzer Hall and I saw a large group of Smiling people helping some people in Wheelchairs with their luggage. I guess we are in the right place. I left all my negative thoughts at home and decided I would make the best of this experience and try to do everything offered and learn as much as I could. I was looking forward to the experience now. Thank you, Cindy. And thank you to all the helpful smiling people that greeted us.

Chapter 10

Day One: Introduction and Orientation

The first people that introduced themselves to me and explained the check-in process were Kelly and Karla. They are two wonderful people.

They had great attitudes and really made me feel comfortable with what was coming and they were good at explaining what was in store for the week. I also sat down with the nurse, Michelle, and went over my medications and any issues I might have. I met with a lot of different people at three different stations. They told me their names, but it was really overwhelming, especially since everyone was wearing masks (leftover Covid19 stuff) so I couldn't see their whole faces. I have a hard time remembering names when I CAN see the face, but when all I can see is the eyes; no way am I going to remember the names. Fortunately, they started wearing name tags (Thank you Ken for that idea!) so I could address everybody by their name rather than "Hey You!" I know now that I met with Mo, Colleen, Carrie, Stephanie (whom I actually recognized from the Empower Hours), Jaclyn, Aleisha, Anna, Kim, Karah, and Liz. I also met Mike (who I had talked with on the phone just a couple days prior) and I think Maggie was with him. Like I said, lots of new faces and names, it was overwhelming to say the least.

While I was going to all the meetings and assessments, Cindy was moving all my supplies, clothes, and other stuff into the Dorm room where I would be staying. They were supposedly Accessible, but they obviously weren't designed by anyone who knew anything about needed space for Wheelchairs. At least one of the two bathrooms had a roll-in shower.

 It was easy to know which room was mine thanks to a sign on my door that Nichole had made for me. Thank You Nichole! The sign was perfect for me. I really like Bison. Big Smiles. I don't know how many trips Cindy made back and forth between my room and our van. I think she had plenty of help. I do know that 3 hours later, after I was done with my meetings, she was still there. I went to my room with her so she could show me where she had stored everything. Boy, the room looked small. Thankfully I didn't spend much time there, only sleeping mostly. I got the feeling Cindy didn't want to leave, but the Empower group assured her that I would be okay and shooed her away. We hugged and kissed and I told her I would call or text when I could. From there I was ushered into the Skaggs building which houses the Physical Therapy program.

In Skaggs Hall we had a buffet style dinner in the entrance area on the first floor of the building. I actually don't remember what we had; I was on information overload at this point.

I met a few people and talked a little. I learned that Liz spoke Portuguese and she recognized my Brasilian accent right away – she speaks Continental Portuguese. That connection helped me feel more comfortable. After dinner we moved into a conference room where we all formed a giant circle so we could, more or less, see everybody. Here we watched a presentation that told us a little about Empower SCI and what we could expect during the following week.

The four directors of the program (Liz Lima, Stephanie Romano, Carrie Callahan, and Monique Dawes) introduced themselves and explained a little of what Empower SCI was all about. After the presentation, we did an "Ice Breaker" where rolls of Toilet Paper were passed around and we were told to take the amount of toilet paper we normally used to clean our bottoms in the bathroom. It turned out that the more squares you took, the more "Facts" about yourself you were to share with the group. That was a funny and entertaining way to start to get to know each other. Again, we were all wearing our Covid masks, so it was hard to put a face to the speaker. I think that lasted until about 10 p.m. or so. By that time, I was ready for bed. Two "Residential Aides" came to my aid and put me to bed. At this point the only way I made transfers in and out of my chair was with a Hoyer lift. Cindy had made sure that Empower had one there in my room for me. Hoyer lifts are no fun to use and this one was a manual lift – no electric assist. Also, the room was really small, so it was hard to maneuver especially with my two-hundred-pound-plus body hanging off the thing. I felt sorry for the two girls trying their best to take care of me. I think it took a good forty-five minutes to get me out of the chair and into the bed and all taken care of. I texted Cindy and let her know I was alright. I slept really well that night.

Chapter 11

Day Two: Lots of New Information and Experiences

I woke up a little after six a.m. The Resident Aides were supposed to show up at six-thirty a.m. to wake me up and get my day started. I just lay in bed waiting. I was anxious to start my first day. I had no idea what was in store for me. They gave us a schedule for the week, but it didn't go into any real detail for me. I didn't really care about the schedule anyway. I figured I would just go where ever they told me to go and do whatever they asked me to do as best I could. I checked my phone for messages and checked my Facebook page to see if anything was going on. Nothing special.

The aides showed up right at six-thirty. They got me dressed and ready for the day. We had to use the Hoyer lift to get me into my chair as I didn't know of any other way to do it at that point. It was an ordeal. The room I was in was very small, so there was no room to really maneuver the Hoyer. The two girls didn't have much experience with the Hoyer. I am not a small guy, around five-foot-eleven and two-hundred-twenty pounds or so. The bed was up against one wall. It was just not an optimal situation. I think it took over an hour of struggling and rolling this way and that just to get me situated in my power chair. The aides were Awesome. They did whatever it took to get the job done and they did not complain one little bit. After getting in my chair, I took my morning pills, brushed my teeth and we, all three, headed over to breakfast at Skaggs Hall.

The tables were packed and everybody was about done. It was eight-thirty and I think we were a little late. I would have to get up earlier if I wanted to make breakfast by eight. After breakfast they had announcements then they sent us off to our individual PT/OT sessions. "Us" refers to the "Participants" of the program. The Participants, of which I was one, were the people who the program was developed to help. We were individuals with some sort of Spinal Cord Injury that were in need of help. There were eight of us: me from Helena, Shelby from Whitefish, Mt, RyanO from Alameda, CA, Andrew, RyanB from Seattle, Tom from Montana City, Gina from Helena, and Ken from Montesano, WA.

This was Ken's second go around with Empower and truthfully probably the reason I was here. Cindy had talked to his wife and she had nothing but good things to say about the program. We talked to Ken and he couldn't say enough about how good the program had been for him. This really motivated Cindy to motivate me to join the program. Whatever made Cindy happy, I would try. Anyway, I was on my way to the next level down where we were to meet for PT. My two aides were with me.

Then Mo accosted me by the elevator and said "we are going to work on things in your room, why don't we just head over there." I said fine, I will go where ever I am directed. We went back to my room. On the first day, I had met with Mo and we had gone over my goals for the Empower program – that is what I was hoping to accomplish during this week with the Empower group. My number one goal was to be able to transfer using a Slide Board. Mo taught me some techniques with the slide board so I could transfer from my chair into bed and back and into the chair from my bed. She gave me some pointers on how to sit up in bed. We transferred to my shower chair out of and into bed. Then we transferred back into my power chair and headed back to Skaggs Hall. That was a lot of work and I was tired. I felt it was good for me though. Down to the lower level of Skaggs Hall and I was in the PT room. There was a lot of equipment I recognized from the other PT places I had been to.

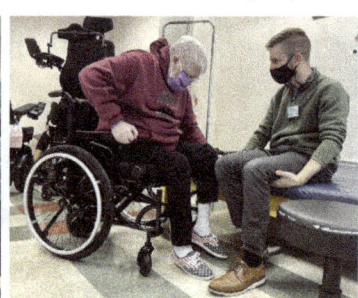

I met with Troy and he was going to work with me on Transfers in and out of the chair. Troy also introduced me to Lionel, who had a few manual chairs with Smart Drives for us to try out. Lionel was nice enough to leave a manual chair for the week so I could use it as much as I wanted. Troy taught me to transfer with the slide board with confidence. After he and Mo were done with me, I didn't need to use the Hoyer lift anymore. In fact, I did not use the Hoyer lift for the rest of the time with Empower SCI Montana 2022. That was Awesome! Troy also took me outside in the manual chair to teach me Wheelchair Skills. I learned a lot from him.

After PT/OT we had lunch on the ground floor of Skaggs Hall. That is where all of our meals would be. The meals were all Buffet style except for the times we had Pizza. I think our first lunch was Grilled Burgers, but I don't really remember. After lunch we had a Therapy session. Only the Participants and the Therapist, Toni, were at this meeting. We would have an hour each day designated for this session. It was a time where we could talk about anything that was bothering us or whatever we felt like we needed to share or get out of our systems. It was a "safe place" for us to feel free to talk and unload.

After our therapy session, we met again in the PT/OT room downstairs where we had a "Show and Tell" session. We got in a big circle again. Everybody took a turn telling about and showing something they used or did to make life in a Wheelchair a little easier. Mike had a large box and a bag of tricks that he had come up with to live a more normal life after his accident. Mike was one of the Peer Mentors that helped us work through issues we might have. Mike lived in Missoula. He also served as an excellent example of what we could do. Matt was the other Peer Mentor. He drove up from Tucson all by himself. He showed us a portable shower chair in a bag. I showed off my drop-front pants (thanks Vickie for all the sewing you have done for me). Tom showed how he used a hay hook to pull up his boots. Lots of interesting stuff was shared.

Dinner followed the show and tell. After dinner we got on a bus and went down to the Water Park in Missoula. We all put life jackets on and got in the pool with several aides by our side. That was the first time since my accident that I had gotten in a swimming pool of any type. The aides had us float on our backs, float on our fronts and roll over in the water. We had to float face down and roll over onto our backs. We also got to swim around. After a little bit we got to take off our life jackets and float around by ourselves. Aides were always right there with us in case we had any issues.

The pool experience felt really good and was a little liberating. We were in the pool about an hour. After that we were taken back to our rooms so we could change. I opted to get out of my wet clothes and have a shower. When I was done with that I just went to bed. It was fairly late, around ten p.m. and I was worn out. I called Cindy to let her know how I was and ask how she was. I slept well that night.

Chapter 12

Day Three: Even More New Experiences

I woke up around five-forty-five the next morning. I tried to go back to sleep, but I couldn't. I suppose I was too excited to see what this day had in store for me. I checked my phone for new texts. My sister Heather usually texts me a good morning every morning. She said she might be flying into Missoula late tonight and have time to visit the next day. I told her we were supposed to go bicycling (tricycling really) at a park in Missoula and maybe she could meet us there. It would be great to see her. Two Residential Aides showed up at six-thirty again right on time. They were cheery and got me taken care of and dressed. They asked if we were going to use the Hoyer to get me into my chair, but I said we should try the Slide Board. We were successful! Yeehaw! I transferred into my chair from the bed pretty much by myself. The aides were right there ready to help (I do think they helped more than they admitted) and make sure I didn't fall flat on my face while trying to make the transfer. It took so much less time that we made breakfast by seven-thirty. Tom and I and our residential aides for the day were the first to show up for breakfast this day.

After breakfast there were announcements, the awarding of the "Golden Gloves" which was a way of acknowledging the outstanding performance by two of the volunteers. That must be hard to decide who deserves the recognition, because every single person involved with Empower was doing an outstanding job. It is incredible that so many people with their own busy careers and lives take the time to volunteer for something like this. They all were very positive and helpful in every way. I never saw anyone complain about anything or balk at doing something that needed done but might not have been very pleasant. Next, we moved downstairs again for Yoga this time. Six aides got together and put me in a "Comfort Carrier" sling to move me out of my chair and onto a Yoga mat on the floor. Strange at first, and I wasn't sure how successful they would be, I mean I am a good-sized guy and not light by any means. They moved me fairly easily though and it felt fine for me.

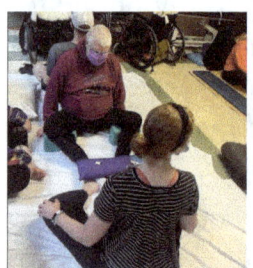 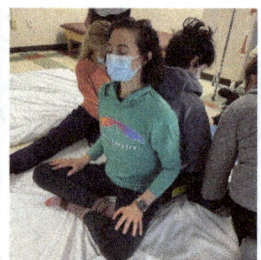 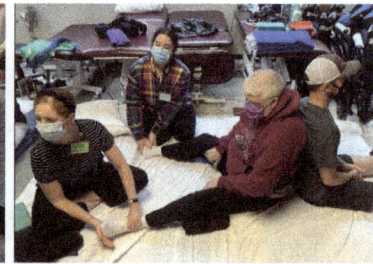

This was the first time since my accident that I had been on the floor. It felt a little weird. The ceiling seemed so far away. The yoga was nice and relaxing – a far cry from the strenuous physical therapy from yesterday. When the Yoga session was over, we had our therapy hour with Toni. Following therapy we had lunch. After lunch, Lionel helped me get used to the Smart Drive on the manual chair. Troy helped a little with some more manual wheelchair skills. We watched a couple presentations on getting closer to a normal life. One topic was adaptive travel, Mike showed us his van that he had modified. It was quite impressive. The next topic was about intimacy and sex. Not all is lost, and just because things don't work like they used to doesn't mean you have to give up on physical intimacy after you become paralyzed.

We had dinner after the presentations. I don't remember what it was, but it was pretty good. Meal times were family style more or less and we got to talking a lot with each other. It provided a good way for participants and aides to mingle and get to know each other. I enjoyed that quite a bit.

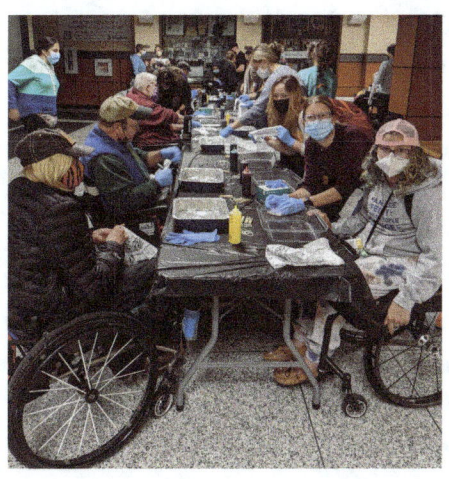

After Dinner we had a Tie-Dye craft session. That was fun. Bandanas or Socks were the choices offered. Rats, if I had known we were going to do this, I would have brought a couple T-shirts from home. I think I have saved seven or eight t-shirts at home to tie-dye, I just haven't gotten around to doing them yet. I had fun anyway. I chose a Bandana and used my three favorite colours: Purple, Green, and Blue. After everybody was done with the Tie-Dye experience, a first for some I think, we were let go to do what we wanted. It was late, around nine, but too early for bed.

I went back to Pantzer Hall and heard a rumor that there were Chocolate Chip Cookies and Milk, and even Chocolate Milk, in the Rec Room downstairs in Pantzer Hall. I followed the lure of the Chocolate down to the Rec Room. Lo and behold there were lots of people in the Rec Room! There were

Chocolate Chip Cookies, Chocolate Chip Fudge Brownies (super delicious), Milk, and a bottle of Hershey's Chocolate Syrup on the table. I was told to help myself.

You don't have to offer twice when Chocolate is involved for me to indulge. I had a couple Chocolate Chip Cookies, they were good. Then I had one of the Chocolate Chip Fudge Brownies and a small cup of Chocolate Milk. One of the aides made the Chocolate Milk for me – thank you so much. The Brownie was excellent and I felt decadent eating it, because I am borderline Type Two diabetic. I have to watch my sugar intake. I knew Cindy might not be happy about the Cookies and the Brownie, but she wasn't here and I had been getting a lot more exercise in the last two days than I normally got. I would just check my blood sugar in the morning when I woke up. Thank you, Empower Crew, for getting the Chocolate desserts.

While we were snacking on the Chocolate Cookies and Brownies, one of the aides got on her phone and brought up the game "Would you Rather . . .?" and we were playing that. It was fun, and an entertaining way to get to know each other better. There was also a Foosball table there. I hadn't played Foosball in quite a while. RyanO wanted to play and it was easy to find a couple other people to join us. Abby and I made up one team and Anita joined RyanO. Abby and I creamed them in the first game (not really, but we did beat them by one point!). The second game we played, RyanO and Anita won by one point. We decided to leave it there, a tie for the night.

That was a really fun evening and it would have been nice to have a little more of that unstructured social time. It had been a very long time since I had been around a group of people just for fun that really paid no attention to the fact that some of us were in wheelchairs. I went to bed around eleven p.m. That was after the aides assigned to me for the evening were supposed to be off shift, but they didn't seem to mind. One of them, Mason, asked if my chair had the "Elevator" function.

It did. He suggested I raise my chair a little when getting into bed with the slide board so I would slide downhill. I did that and it was extremely easier. Why didn't I think of that before. It worked great! Thank you, Mason. After they put me to bed, I fell asleep right away.

Chapter 13

Day Four: Cycling is My High Point!

Again, I woke up around six a.m. And again, I couldn't fall back asleep. I texted good morning to Heather and waited for my aides to arrive. They showed up right at six-thirty again. They got me quickly dressed and loaded into the chair and we were off to Breakfast with Tom. Again, we were the first to show up. Same deal as yesterday – breakfast, announcements, awarding of the Golden Gloves, and off to our assignment for the morning. I started off with Mo again for OT in my room.

First thing was to transfer into my bed from the chair. I told her about the trick Mason had mentioned, about raising the chair so I could slide downhill into bed, but she said "Oh, No! We are not doing that here. You can use the tricks at home, but here we are going to work, Work, WORK to get it right!" Okay, whatever you say Mo. That may sound a little strict, but it was great. If I could do it the hard way, then the easy way would just be that much easier. Thank you, Mo. Mo also taught me some techniques, for putting on pants or shorts mostly by myself.

After she was done with me, we went back to Skaggs Hall and I was handed over to Troy. We worked on more manual wheelchair skills. Troy took me to a grassy spot outside and we worked on doing wheelies. That is kind of like riding a unicycle for me, takes more balance than I have. I will have to work on that quite a bit to get it down. We had pizza for lunch. My sister, Heather, showed up for lunch. She had spent the night in Missoula and her flight out didn't leave until six or so in the evening so she got to spend the afternoon with us.

That was great, because after lunch we loaded up in buses and went to a park in Missoula where Julie from DREAM Adaptive Recreation had a bunch of hand-powered tricycles for us to try out. There was also Peter Pauwels who had brought a bunch of adaptive fishing gear for us to try out. The fishing gear was interesting but I was really interested in the hand-powered cycles. Julie even had an all-electric powered cycle that looked more like an electric dirt bike to me. It looked like fun, but you wouldn't get much exercise riding it. The Empower crew used the Comfort Carrier to put me into the hand-powered cycle. Julie explained how everything worked, shifting gears, the electric assist, steering two different ways, braking.

I told her I didn't use brakes because all they do is slow you down! Then she went on a little ride with me and a couple others from the Empower group. We just rode on the bike trail around the park. It was great fun and good exercise.

After the ride I got back in the manual wheelchair. I teamed up with Phoebe and we played a couple games of corn hole against Liz and Mo. Liz and Mo beat us the first time, but Phoebe and I pulled out a win for the second game, thanks to Phoebe, not me. It was lots of fun.

We went back to Skaggs Hall for dinner after we were done at the park. Everybody was happy and talking about what a great experience the cycling was. After dinner we were supposed to have a therapy session with Toni. We went to a Baseball game instead. That was probably good therapy for us too. The weather was fantastic and the evening was warm. We had a good time at the game. I enjoyed talking with Jasmine and RyanB more than watching the game.

Jasmine, RyanB, and I were sitting on the third baseline. A Lefty was up to bat and hit a foul ball that came whizzing right by RyanB's head, I swear it only missed her face by a few inches. It surprised the heck out of us, it happened so fast. It ended up hitting the guy sitting next to RyanB in his shoulder. Some young kid ran over and grabbed the ball, didn't even give it to the old guy that got hit. Anyway, we had a good time. We left before the game was over and I think the only one upset about that was Tom. Not because we were leaving early, but because just at the time we were leaving, the bases were loaded and the batter that was up was known for hitting home runs. It looked like the team was about to score four runs. I don't know how it turned out. We got back to Pantzer Hall and I just went to bed. We'd had a pretty physically demanding day and I was tired.

Chapter 14

Day Five: A Day at the Lake

I woke up at a quarter to six again. I was well rested and ready for another day! My aides for the day showed up at six-thirty and got me dressed, loaded, and to Skaggs Hall by seven-thirty again. Not using the Hoyer was fabulous. It saves so much time and is so much easier on my handlers and easier on me. No one has to struggle with that thing and I don't have to be rolled every which way and left hanging while I am moved around. Breakfast was the same buffet style. We had the same announcements, Golden Gloves presentation, and a short explanation of what we were doing today.

We started off with Yoga. It was relaxing again. We learned a few new techniques. Right after Yoga we loaded into cars and vans. RyanO and I got into a minivan driven by Gavin from the Montana Independent Living Project. Liz and Emily joined us. Gavin was into Motorcycles; he rode one all the time. RyanO was into Harleys and had owned several, and I of course, love Motorcycles and Sidecar Rigs. RyanO rode shotgun and I was right behind him in the middle of the van. Liz and Emily sat in the row of seats at the back of the van. We were going to Placid Lake, just over an hour away. Of course, our conversation during the ride was mostly about Motorcycles. I think Liz fell asleep. Emily talked a little about Motorcycles but said she didn't really care for them even though her boyfriend rode one. The drive passed by quickly, I didn't even see the Giant Cow when we turned off Highway two hundred at the Clearwater Junction onto Highway eighty-three to Seeley Lake.

I had ridden this road many times, but had never visited the park at Placid Lake. It was a very nice place. By the time we got there, Julie from DREAM Adaptive Recreation and Peter Pauwels, the same two who had let us use their equipment at the park in Missoula just two days ago, had their boats unloaded and were getting set up to introduce us to boating with handicaps. Steve Smith from Hydrologistics Montana also had some boats. It was amazing how many boats were lined up for our use. Everybody unloaded and we had a little introduction and orientation as to how the day was going to go. After that we had a Picnic Lunch; sandwiches, chips, pop. After lunch we loaded into the boats we wanted to try out.

The first boat I went in was a Drift Boat that had been adapted to be wheelchair accessible by Hydrologistics Montana. It was awesome. The back flipped down and doubled as a ramp to drive the wheelchair right into the boat. The seats came out easily so I could drive right up to the front of the boat then the seats were replaced, the back was flipped back up, locked into place and we were off.

After my excursion in the Drift Boat, I got to try out a Kayak. I was loaded into the Kayak with the Comfort Carrier again. I was transferred into the Kayak on land then carried into the water, kayak and all. After I was in the water, Mason hopped in the back and we were off. It was great fun and the first time

since the mid-eighties that I had been in a kayak. It was good exercise and more than my shoulder was used to since my accident. It was a good thing Mason was in the back or I may not have made it back! Everybody had such a great time that we stayed longer than originally planned.

The sun was going down by the time we got back to the University of Montana campus. We had dinner when we got back. Was it pizza again? I don't really remember; I was still pretty high from the afternoon at the lake. We got our tie-dye items back. They turned out pretty well. I liked my Bandana. I rolled it up and put it on. I went back to my room and took a shower with the help of my aides. I made a comparatively early night of it and went to bed after my shower. Tomorrow would be our last day of activities.

Chapter 15

Day Six: Preparing Food and Closing Ceremonies

I woke up a little after six this morning. I must have been pretty tired from yesterday's activities. I slept well. My aides showed up at six-thirty, prompt as usual. They got me ready, dressed, in my chair and at Breakfast by seven-thirty again. Not as many people showed up this morning. After Breakfast we had the normal announcements and Golden Gloves awarded. Then Mo, who teaches Occupational Therapy and brought two of her students with her to the Empower Camp,

told us that today for PT/OT we would be doing a project put together by her two students, Sammi and Bre.

They had come up with a Food Preparation and Kitchen Skills project for all of us to work on together. Mike had generously offered the use of his Kitchen in his own home. Awesome, Mike! Thank you. I wanted to see how Mike had his house set up. We piled into a bunch of cars, Anita had rented an accessible van that she drove RyanO and me over to Mike's place in. I don't really know how everybody else got there, but by the time we rolled in, Sammi and Bre and the other aides had work stations set up for us. RyanO worked on Quesadillas and Shelby helped him after she diced up some Tomatoes for me.

I scooped and mushed Avocados into a bowl. I diced Onions, squeezed a little Lemon into it added some spices, and mixed it all together with the Tomatoes diced by Shelby to make Guacamole. Ken and RyanB were hard at work making Apple Tarts. They had to peel the Apples and chop them up. They also had to make a piecrust and put it all in a muffin tin. They were baked in Mike's Pellet Cooker outside on his patio. It looked like they were having fun, even if it was hard work.

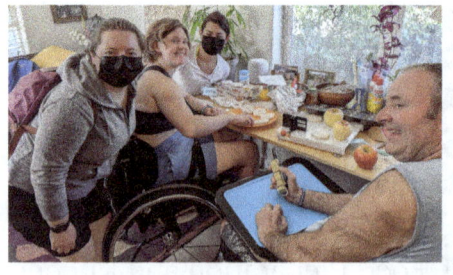

This was a fantastic activity. It was lots of fun, brought everybody together, and we all had some good things to eat when we were done. Mike's dog, Bodhi, kept an eye on all of us while we were at his place. He is a great dog and friendly too. He knows his way around a wheelchair too. Big Smiles.

I got a photo of the Three Sams in the program. Samantha and Sammi were Residential Aides. They are fabulous people. When we were all done, we headed back to Skaggs Hall with all the food we had just prepared for lunch. Troy drove me and RyanO back in the van that Anita had rented. I rode shotgun! It was the first time since my accident that I have ridden in the front of a vehicle and the first time I could actually see out like a normal passenger since I have been wheelchair bound. It was Great! After lunch we had our last Therapy session with Toni. It was a beautiful day – Sunny and warm – so we held it outside on the Grass under a Big Tree, like the place where Alice in Wonderland's sister read to her and started the whole trip down the rabbit hole. At the end of this week, I felt like I was coming up and out of the Rabbit Hole I had fallen down after my accident. I didn't see any White Rabbits.

Next, we gathered in one of the Conference rooms in Skaggs Hall and participated in the Closing Ceremonies. Here we got to share about our progress and whether or not we felt we had accomplished what we had hoped to accomplish going through this program. We passed around a ball of String, whoever had the string had the floor. When the person holding the string was finished, they had to choose one person who had been the biggest influence or impact on themself during that week, then pass the string to that person. I did not really like this part. I liked sharing my feelings and thoughts about the program, but I did Not like having to choose just one person.

Everybody was such a great influence and everybody helped me improve my situation and myself. I mean, how do you choose out of thirty-eight people just One?! And that's not even counting the Seven other Participants! Ken is the main reason, besides Cindy, that I even decided to try this program out. The positivity and growth I saw in each of the other Participants was a huge plus for me. Choose just one person, yeah right. I wanted Forty-five balls of string so I could pass one to every other person involved in this program. The Closing Ceremonies were sad too, because it meant that our experience with Empower was just about done. I would definitely be staying in touch with these people who had so positively affected my life. Even though we had spent only one week together, we had gotten to know each other fairly well and it felt like my family had grown.

After that meeting, we loaded into buses and headed to dinner at a restaurant. We went to Conflux for dinner. They had prepared a very nice Buffet style dinner for us. There were plenty of options and the food was very good. The company was better.

After dinner, a Rumour was spreading quickly through the ranks that we would be going for Montana made Ice Cream at the Big Dipper. I wonder who started that Rumour? I know I helped spread it, Impishly Smiling. The Rumour must have been true, because we loaded back on the buses and headed to the Big Dipper Ice Cream Parlour. Yumm, Yumm. It's hard to lick your lips and smile at the same time. The line was long when we got to the Big Dipper, but that was okay. We were all enjoying the conversation and each other's company.

I imagine the Big Dipper almost sold out of Huckleberry Ice Cream. I had a Waffle Cone with Huckleberry and Mexican Chocolate, it was Delicious! When we finished our Ice Cream we walked back to Pantzer Hall. It was about a mile and the longest trip I had ever made in my wheelchair. I would have been worn out if  I had been using a manual wheelchair. I need one to get more exercise. Hopefully I will be getting one soon. It was dark and time for bed when we got back. I slept really good, but I was not looking forward to the next day. We would be leaving and going back home. At least Cindy would be there to pick me up. I missed her.

Chapter 16

Day Seven: Parting Ways

I woke up around six a.m. for the last time. The aides showed up at six-thirty for the last time. They prepped me for the day and got me into my chair and we headed to Breakfast for the last time. Tom was a little ways behind us. We got to Skaggs Hall for breakfast by seven-thirty again. Hardly anyone was there. There were no announcements, no Golden Gloves awards, the program was basically over.

I suppose many of the people were packing up and getting ready to leave rather than have one last family-style breakfast. After I was done eating, I saw Mo and RyanO talking. I went to join them. Mo was giving RyanO an exit interview. She said she would get together with me after she was done with RyanO. I was

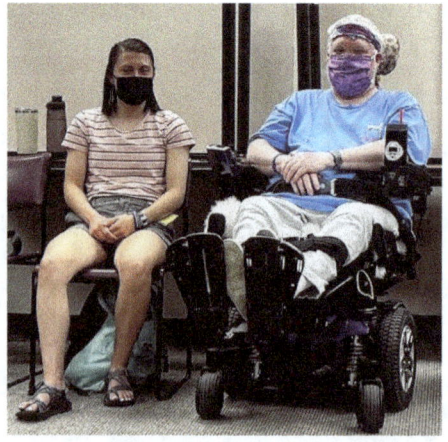

also to meet with Maggie and have an exit interview with her. She videoed the interview and just asked a few questions about what I had expected, what goals I had made and how successful I thought I had been in meeting those goals. She asked how I felt about the program, the people involved, and whether or not I felt it had helped me. I told her I thought it was an excellent program with exceptional people and it had helped me immensely with both skills and emotional health. Like Ken, I couldn't say enough about how good I felt the program was and how much it has helped me.

Next, I had an exit interview with Kim. She had a form to fill out with my responses to a set of questions about how I felt about the program, whether or not I felt I had been successful in meeting the goals I had set and whether or not I thought the program was time well spent. Of Course, I felt the program was time well spent. I felt I had exceeded the goals I had set. I had the same interview again with Mo. The people were wonderful and I will miss them all. When I was done with the interviews, I saw Cindy had arrived and was just about done packing all my stuff into our van. She had plenty of help from the aides still there.

It was good to see Cindy. She finished packing our van, then I introduced her to some of the people who were still there. Ken's son was there to pick up Ken. I had met him the night before at our dinner.

RyanO's brother was there. He arrived on the day we went to the lake so he could spend some time with RyanO. Tom's wife was there too. Cindy exchanged phone numbers with her so we could get together at a later date. I got some photos and said good-byes to everybody. Cindy loaded me into our van and we were off, heading back home to Helena. I had gotten everybody's contact info and plan on staying in touch with them. I am looking forward to seeing many of them again next year.

Empower SCI 2022 Montana. It was an incredible, life-changing experience for me. I met so many fabulous people. Thank you to everyone involved and especially those who talked me into going; Cindy, Ken, and Mike. I am So glad I didn't back out. Big Smiles.

Acknowledgements

I would like to thank my wife, Cindy, for all her love, care, and motivation. Without her, I probably wouldn't be here and definitely wouldn't have written this book.

I would like to thank the Paramedics who scraped me off the Highway and got me to the UAB Hospital. Without them and their promptness, I surely would not be here.

I would like to thank the staff at the University Alabama Birmingham Hospital. For the most part they did a very good job repairing me and taking care of me. I would especially like to thank the Nurse, Blessing Emenyonu. She went above and beyond her duties taking care of me and teaching Cindy how to take care of me for when we would leave the Hospital.

I would like to thank my family (and Cindy's family whom I consider to be my family as well) who keeps supporting me and visiting me even though I haven't been able to visit them like I used to. You help me keep my spirits up and keep me in an emotionally healthy and stable place.

I would like to thank those friends of mine who keep in touch and visit me when they can - you know who you are. You keep my spirits up and help me remember why it is better to be on this side of the dirt rather than pushing up Daisies!

I would like to thank Julie from DREAM Adaptive Recreation in Missoula, Montana for bringing the cycles and boats for the Empower group to use. Also thank you to Peter Pauwels fishwithpeter@gmail.com for bringing his fishing gear and boats.

www.dreamadaptive.org
Dream Adaptive Recreation, Inc.
P.O. Box 4084
Whitefish, Montana
59937 406-862-1817

I would like to thank Steve Smith with Hydrologistics Montana for his Drift Boat Experience. He can be reached at 406-203-7150 or hydrologistics4df@gmail.com

Finally, I would like to thank ALL the people at Empower SCI, especially the Directors: Carrie Callahan, Liz Lima Remillard, Jessica Goodine, Monique Dawes, and Stephanie Romano. They have a superb program that helps people in my condition more than they realize, I am sure. Two people who deserve special recognition are Karla Feitl and Kelly Pantason. They worked tirelessly to make sure the Empower Camp Montana 2022 was a success.

www.empowersci.org
Empower Spinal Cord Injury
P.O.Box 582
Warren, RI 02886

About the Author

sam humphrey

Sam lives in Helena, Montana with his lovely and hardworking wife, Cindy, and their two cats, Spook and Boo. He still loves Motorcycles and hopes to get back in the Wind. He spends his time reading, writing, doing craft projects and puzzles. He enjoys a good game of Chess or Backgammon when he can find a worthy opponent.

Other Books by this Author

WET PAY
Stories from my Career as a Commercial Diver

www.ingramcontent.com/pod-product-compliance
Lightning Source LLC
Chambersburg PA
CBHW071158120626
46546CB00006B/2328